Why Me Lord?

Why Me Lord?

*The Amelia Sambula Story
Turning Tragedy Into Triumph*

Daniel J. Cabot

Copyright © 2013 by Daniel J. Cabot.

ISBN:	Softcover		978-1-4797-9260-3
	Ebook			978-1-4797-9261-0

All rights reserved. No part of this book may be reproduced or transmitted in any form or by any means, electronic or mechanical, including photocopying, recording, or by any information storage and retrieval system, without permission in writing from the copyright owner.

Scripture is quoted from New King James Version.

This book was printed in the United States of America.

Rev. date: 08/30/2013

To order additional copies of this book, contact:
Xlibris LLC
1-888-795-4274
www.Xlibris.com
Orders@Xlibris.com
130265

CONTENTS

Acknowledgements...9
Foreword...13

1	Go West Young Man	15
2	The Wonder Years...	19
3	Sixteen Candles...	24
4	Calling All Angels...	35
5	An Angel is Called Home—11.22.69	38
6	Innocent Blood	46
7	Calling Hours 2 to 4 and 7 to 9	50
8	Home for the Holidays...	53
9	Players To Be Named Later......................................	55
10	Our Father Who Art in Heaven	57
11	See You on the Other Side.......................................	59
12	One Year Later	62
13	Lightning Strikes Again—09.17.75	66
14	George and AA..	68
15	Carol and AA	73
16	Love Is In The Air	78
17	The Angels Rejoice	84
18	Twenty Years Later	86
19	Villa Angela Honor Roll..	91
20	The Power of Prayer	95
21	Forgiveness..	98
22	03.20.11...	101
23	It Is Well With My Soul	103
24	In a Mind's Eye	106
25	300 Paces, 28 seconds, 10 Feet	108
26	God Doesn't Discriminate	111
27	Cousin Jerry..	113
28	A Visit to Amy	117
29	The Beginning..	124

This book is dedicated to our Lord and Savior who is our rock. We also dedicate this book to our former Pastor Robert Murphey and our current Pastor Robert Majetich who have provided us with love, guidance and mentoring as our spiritual leaders. It is our sincere hope that you find this book to be a source of comfort when those storm billows blow. In His love—George and Carol Sambula and Daniel Cabot.

ACKNOWLEDGEMENTS

I have an entire cast of players I would like to acknowledge here so please indulge me for a minute. First of all I'd like to acknowledge my earthly parents, Daniel V. and Jean B. Cabot (both deceased). While the salvation message was never formally preached in our household (primarily given to the fact that we were practicing Catholics—and not too often at that) I have often witnessed my father kiss a cross of Jesus as he said his evening prayers. I really can't say whether or not he and my mother were ever saved by the blood of Jesus, but I do know that they did provide me with a strong moral compass and a puritanical work ethic. I don't know whether or not I will see them in glory and, that does sadden me, but I do thank God for giving me Daniel V. and Jean B. Cabot as earthly role models. God certainly could have done far worse by me.

I'd like to acknowledge my second set of earthly parents, Paul and Kathryn Beyer (my in-laws who are now both deceased). They, along with my brothers-in-law Paul and Rick, my sister-in-law Kathy and their spouses, my assorted nieces and nephews, have, as an only child, given me a sense of family and are the role models of what a Christian family should be. They, along with their sister Patty, my wife of 30+ years, have shown me unconditional love well before I deserved it and well before I invited Christ into my heart. The entire family was most Christ-like in their love for me as well as other members of the extended Beyer family. That tradition carries on to this day and will into the future as well.

I'd like to acknowledge the individuals who prayed the Holy Spirit into my heart. I know for a fact that my wife Patty, my cousin Louis Cabot, Elder Paul Shank, and countless others prayed for my salvation long before I made a decision for Christ. I'd like to thank Pastor Bob Sepkovich who started the Gospel House Rap in Bedford, Ohio in the 1970's, where I first heard the Gospel message preached on a Thursday night in the early 1980's. I can fondly recall (we were quite lo-tech back then) a transparency shown on the wall of the song "Jesus, Jesus, Jesus, there is something about that name" as several hundred of us sang off key each Thursday night. That was my first inkling that I needed Christ in my heart.

I'd like to mention an unnamed evangelist preacher who came to Bedford Bible Baptist Church in March of 1983 and gave a salvation message I shall never forget. I fondly remember going to church with my wife Patty that day and my nine year old son, Kenwyn. Often times Patty and Kenwyn would go on their own as I wanted nothing to do with those Jesus freaks. I was just fine the way I was. On that Sunday morning in particular this unnamed evangelist just happened to be at Bedford Bible Baptist Church and I happened to decide to go to church just one more time. That evangelist gave a salvation message about bridges (i.e. Golden Gate Bridge, London Bridge, Brooklyn Bridge, etc.) and said that Jesus Christ was the bridge between here and heaven and all we had do was to admit we were sinners and invite Christ into our hearts. The next thing I knew was in front of 150 or so people I never saw before, I answered that altar call and invited Christ into my heart. It goes without saying that my life has never been the same since.

I want to personally acknowledge George and Carol Sambula and their family. I know that for George and his offspring my writing this book has not been easy for them. At one time during the creation of this book, we passed Amelia's 41st anniversary of her home going (November 22, 1969). All writing ceased for a moment as George needed time to gather himself. We began again around Christmas of 2010 and again this was a time of sorrow and painful reflection for George and his children as I am sure 40+ years of memories are as real as if the advent of Amelia's death was yesterday.

Finally, I would be remiss if I did not mention God, His loving Son and the Holy Spirit here. God has given me the talent to put His thoughts on paper here. Through the Holy Spirit He has provided me with a number of 5:00 AM wake-up calls with various bits and pieces of inspiration to add to this work. God has given all of us His only Son as a redeeming Savior who cleanses us of all our sins. He has given us the knowledge that like Amelia to be absent from the body is to be present with the Lord. He has given us the promise for those of us who have admitted we are sinners and have invited Christ into our hearts, we will spend eternity in Heaven with those we love. I would also like to give special acknowledgement to Sally Johnson who tirelessly proofread this text for me on more than one occasion. I'd like to also note that all scripture quoted in this book is taken from the New King James version of the Bible.

FOREWORD

Why me Lord? is much more than a book about the senseless taking of a life. It is a book about forgiveness and grace. It is the story of the life of George Sambula whose daughter was taken from him on November 22, 1969 at age seventeen through a tragic and senseless crime. It is the story of how George's grief led to alcoholism and a continued downward spiral ending with the subsequent loss of his first wife.

This book is also about God's grace and mercy and his continual love for George and how God took a series of tragedies in George's life and created a new man full of grace and love and forgiveness. It is the story of how George met a new love of his life, Carol, through Alcoholics Anonymous and how they both walked together healing each other and sharing God's love along the way.

Come with me as we explore what God has done in the lives of George and Carol. As we turn each page together let us remember that life is not a footrace but a marathon and that God is in control and he has a special path for each of us which we must dutifully walk until we get to Glory.

Amelia (Amy) Sambula wrote the following words on October 24, 1969 less than a month away from her untimely demise. Perhaps she knew her time was near and wanted to share the following message of love and grace with those she would soon leave behind:

"To me, religion is the belief in a loving triune God: God the Father, God the Son, and God the Holy Spirit. It is the belief that God lives and works in and through me by my own choice. It is my meaning in life that I scarcely comprehend, but as a Christian I yearn to understand self by realizing God's presence in me and in others. I believe that God sent his

Son, who died for me and through His death brought a great power of love to all men. It is only through the Son we can go to the Father and it is by the Holy Spirit we are enlightened to eternal life."

Amy Sambula
October 24, 1969

> She's a good girl. Loves her mama
> She loves Jesus and America, too

From "I'm Free" by Tom Petty and the Heartbreakers

> Indescribable, uncontainable,
> You placed the stars in the sky
> And you know them by name.
> You are amazing God.
> All powerful, untamable,
> Awesome we fall to our knees
> As we humbly proclaim, You are amazing God.

Chorus from "Indescribable"

CHAPTER ONE

Go West Young Man

Whenever I am afraid, I will trust in you.
In God (I will praise his word),
In God I have put my trust; I will not fear.
What can flesh do to me?

Psalm 56:3-4

Charles Dickens once said that it was the best of times and it was the worst of times. In Cleveland, Ohio in 1962 it was the best of times for a young man seeking his fame and fortune. Jobs were plentiful. All you had to do was fill out an application and you could work at the local steel mills or the local automotive plants or work with one of the local utilities and do quite well for yourself. Overtime was plentiful and the cost of living was more than reasonable. The top three automobile makers were still king. General Motors owned over 60% of the domestic car market and the upstart manufacturers with names such as Honda and Toyota were laughable at best. We would never imagine back then that one day we would ever say that Toyota was the number one selling automobile manufacturer in the world. A nice new shiny Chevrolet Impala or Ford Galaxy or Plymouth Fury car would set you back less than $2,500.00 and for a couple of hundred bucks you could upgrade to a new Buick or Pontiac or Mercury. Gas was thirty cents a gallon (and there was such a thing as full service) and you could buy a new home for under $20,000.00. You could buy five loaves of bread for under a dollar (if you wanted to) and milk was a dollar a gallon and a postage stamp set you back a whopping four cents.

Neighborhoods in Cleveland were well preserved and neighbors looked out for each other and all was well with the world.

And so in the Summer of 1962 George Sambula decided to head west. West out of Pennsylvania, that is. He did set his sights on the West Coast—he did not even cross the Mississippi. He did not even cross the Cuyahoga River—the watery border separating the Eastern half of Cleveland proper from its Western brethren. He settled on the shores of Lake Erie just as Moses Cleaveland did so many years ago—I believe that Moses had actually spelled his last name Cleaveland.

George had two major goals in mind when he made his solo trek to the big city. One, he was looking for stable employment. He was born in Charleroi, PA on December 9, 1931 and graduated from high school in 1950. Like his forefathers George was left with two choices—the mills or the mines. George had most recently worked for Pittsburgh Steel and had been laid off half the time during his five year tenure at the mill. Two, George knew that he had a drinking problem and so he felt that leaving his drinking buddies behind would help resolve that issue in his life.

When George elected to leave for Cleveland his wife Joan was expecting their 5th child and so George left his family behind until the birth of their child. George loaded up his 1959 Chevrolet Impala and headed off for parts unknown.

Upon arriving in the big city George was befriended by Stanley Neuman and his family who took him in while he searched for work and housing. According to George, Stanley and his family were like family to George's parents and his immediate family.

George found work at King Musical Instruments making valves and pistons for musical instruments. He was happy to have a job and not to have to worry about being laid off any more. George would drive home back to Pennsylvania each and every weekend, working weekdays on the shop floor.

While George's first goal (i.e. steady employment) was easily achieved his second goal of stopping drinking was not that easy to accomplish. George loved to go to the Two Crows Bar on E. 185th Street. It was his favorite watering hole. George knew that he had a drinking problem but did not know what else to do. The Two Crows happened to be within walking distance where he first settled and he could drink to his heart's content and walk back home. Very convenient.

In the Spring of 1963 George and his family were reunited. No more lonely nights. No more having to go to the bars to drink those lonely nights away. George was a new father when Kathleen Sambula was born in March of 1963. All was right with the world now. Eleven year old Amelia (Amy) along with nine year old James and eight year old George and three year old Annette along with Mom and baby Kathleen were all one big happy family again.

George and Joan began searching for a new home and settled on one at Pawnee Avenue (off of E. 185th) in Cleveland, Oh. It was near the shores of Lake Erie and the house was in a very good location with it being close to schools, church, and shopping. Of course, their new abode was also within walking distance to the Two Crows Bar and soon George was one of the regulars once again. Old habits die hard.

Amelia (Amy) Sambula

Amy was eleven years old when she and her family were reunited in March of 1963. She had blonde curly hair with bright blue eyes and stood about 5'2". Her Uncle Bill had nicknamed her "blue eyes."

The move at first was very hard for Amelia. Kids could be especially cruel in the 5th grade and the kids at her Catholic elementary school were no exception. The kids at first did not accept Amelia and she wanted to go back home and live with Grandma. Amelia's mother Joan talked Amelia off of the ledge and Amelia did adjust over time. There was no doubt in George's mind his little girl was special—that God had a special plan for her and that her initial school problems were soon overcome as Amelia continued to lean upon God for her daily strength.

George and Joan and all the kids attended mass every Sunday at Our Lady of Perpetual Help Church. George had heard about Jesus Christ from the messages from the pulpit but had no idea what it meant to invite Jesus into his life as his personal savior. The drinking continued and things were alright with the world.

Carol Zimmerman

As George was busy making a life for himself and his family, Carol had turned 18 years old and was a proud member of the Shaw High School class of 1962. She was still living at home with her parents and her sister on Nelaview in East Cleveland, Ohio. She had dreams of getting married, having children, and living in a house with a white picket fence and living happily ever after.

After graduation Carol started working at Huron Road Hospital in the X-Ray department as a receptionist and a secretary. She was single and dated on and off but had no steady boyfriend at the time. She was happy and content and spent a lot of time hanging out with her friends. Carol enjoyed swimming, ice and roller skating and dancing. She loved the popular music of her time and listening to top ten hits such as "He's So Fine" by the Chiffons and "Walk Like a Man" by Frankie Valli and the Four Seasons and "Dominique" by the Singing Nun.

In 1963 Carol and her friends starting hanging out at Happy's Bar on E. 152nd and Lakeshore Boulevard. It was a young crowd and they would go there a couple of times a week. At first Carol did not want to go in there with her friends. The first time they went there Carol stayed in the car. The next time they went there Carol was talked into going in by her friends. Carol had hated the bar scene. Her dad used to go to bars and she hated even the thought of going out drinking. However, once Carol started going to Happy's she felt better about herself. Her sense of inadequacy and lack of self worth seemed to magically disappear. Carol spent the next thirteen years of her life as a regular at Happy's. Somehow, her resident stool at Happy's really did not do much to permanently solve those issues of self-worth and self-esteem. She had no idea of what the Lord had in store for her as the years rolled along.

The ironic thing here is that George and Carol's favorite watering holes were less than five minutes away by automobile—yet their lives might have been a million miles apart until their paths eventually crossed through the loving grace of Christ and His Father.

CHAPTER TWO

The Wonder Years

Back in the 1980's there was a television show known as the Wonder Years which depicted life in the 1960's from a young man entering his teen years. We now look into the lives of George and Amy and Carol as the calendar crosses over from 1964 to 1965 as Amy begins her initial road to emancipation as she is about to enter that magical age of 13—sort of stuck between the end of childhood and the beginning of womanhood. That magical date was February 20, 1965.

George

Things were going well for George as America had buried President Kennedy and was still adjusting to the Presidency of Lyndon B. Johnson and fighting a war in Southeast Asia. George was doing well at King Instruments. He has progressed from the machine department to the valve department where he did a great deal of precision hand work including soldering of intricate parts for precision musical instruments. George liked his job and did his job well and was well liked by both his co-workers and his bosses. George seemed a million miles away from the steel mills of his old home town where labor was grueling and layoffs were always around the corner.

Things were looking good for George and his family as they christened the new year coming into 1965. George was very proud of his wife Joan and his big family. His house was well kept and he took care of any small repairs that needed to be tended to as the man of the house. George took his role as both a husband and father very seriously and did all he could to be a good husband and provider. He loved Joan and the kids and marveled at how big everybody was getting. Amy was the oldest as she was approaching that magical age of 13 followed by Jim and George then Annette and finally Kathy. Both he and Joan were active in a Fathers and Mothers Club which brought a host of new friends into their home.

In 1964 George and Joan went down to Jackshaw Chevrolet on E. 185th Street and bought a brand new four door green 1964 Chevrolet Impala sedan. George walked past the Corvettes and hot rod 409 Chevy two door Impalas and bought just what he and his family needed—a sensible family car as American as apple pie and the flag.

George and his family were Catholics and were still attending Our Lady of Perpetual Help Church every Sunday. George knew who Jesus was but had not yet invited Him into his heart as his personal savior.

George and the boys at the Two Crows were still hard at it in 1964. George visited his drinking buddies there on a daily basis and drank either Iron City Beer or draft beer. Ironically George used to smoke Lucky Strikes but quit smoking because smoking interfered with his drinking. He would rather drink than smoke. George enjoyed fishing near his home on Lake Erie and was an accomplished pool player and bowling machine aficionado. George considered himself to be a controlled drinker and would never think of putting his drinking ahead of his family. Still he could not resist the allure of the boys at the Two Crows. George could never imagine that one day beer would never touch his lips again.

Amelia (Amy)

As Amy was approaching her 13th birthday in the spring of 1965 she still carried sadness in her heart over the assassination of President Kennedy. Like many persons of her age they saw for perhaps the first time a great tragedy play out on national television. They saw a vibrant young charming leader of the free world cut down before their very eyes. The author himself can recall to this day where he was and what he was doing as the news broke regarding the assassination of President Kennedy. It was something that will stay with us of the baby boomer generation forever.

Things were still tough for Amy at her new school as she progressed from age 12 to 13. The teasing and taunting caused Amy to try even harder which resulted in her becoming a straight A student. Amy was going to Oliver Hazard Perry (one of Cleveland's public schools) and she was an excellent trumpet player. Amy loved to play "The Impossible Dream" with her trumpet and it was her father's favorite song. Amy loved history and parliamentary procedures. She also loved Asian studies and was a great debater and a leader at school. Amy was well liked by her teachers and her principal.

Despite the initial adjustment period, Amy had many friends and was well liked by both her friends and her family. Amy was very outgoing and loving. Even at the tender age of 13 George and Joan knew that Amy had the Spirit of Jesus in her. Her friends knew that Amy prayed to the Lord Jesus Christ. They would write to her for advice and asked her to pray for them. Amy would take time to answer all of the letters she received and took time to pray when called upon to do so. All of her friends knew that Amy had Christ in her heart and wanted what she had. She helped many of her friends find Christ. Amy's favorite prayer was the Prayer to St. Francis of Assisi which says the following:

> LORD, make me an instrument of Your peace;
> Where there is hatred, let me sow love;
> Where there is injury, pardon;
> Where there is doubt, faith;
> Where there is despair, hope;
> Where there is darkness, light;
> And where there is sadness, joy.
>
> O, Divine Master, grant that I seek not so much
> to be consoled, but to console;
> To be understood, as to understand;
> To be loved, as to love;
> For it is in giving that we receive;
> It is in pardoning that we are pardoned;
> And it is in dying that we are born to eternal life.

Neither George nor Joan would ever dream that a few short years later they would be called upon to put each and every one of these words to the ultimate test.

Carol Zimmerman

The dawning of 1965 found Carol with mixed emotion. Like the rest of the country, she was still saddened by the loss of President Kennedy. Carol was working her part-time job at Higbees when the President was assassinated. She was working in the jewelry and hosiery departments which were right next to the TV department. Shoppers from all over the store were glued to those television sets watching the news of the death of President Kennedy.

In 1964 Carol's grandmother died and that left a big hole in Carol's heart. Carol was still living at home and her grandmother also lived with Carol and her parents. Carol and her grandmother were very close. Carol felt a kinship with her grandmother and felt very blessed to have her. Carol remembers that her grandmother used to sit in her rocker with her Bible and her eyes closed. Carol thought that she was sleeping but came to find out that she was praying. Eventually Carol would come to know the power of prayer in her life.

In 1965, in Carol's social life, she was in a "part-time" relationship that would last for ten years. In her work life, in addition to working evenings at Higbee's, Carol was still working full-time at Huron Road Hospital. She was happy and always on the go with her friends.

Carol bought her first new car, a silver Chevrolet Corvair convertible and she and her friends spent many a summer night in 1965 listening to the radio and cruising the Euclid Manners Big Boy Restaurant. They would listen to the tunes of the day on AM 1260 or AM 1420 out of Cleveland or AM 850 CLKW out of the Motor City and just cruise and cruise and cruise. Life was good in 1964.

Carol and her friends were still regulars at Happy's Bar stopping in two to three times a week. Her favorite drink was scotch. As with many of us who had not yet invited Christ in our hearts, Carol was seeking to fill that emptiness in her soul that could not be filled at Happy's or anywhere else. Carol was still on a long and winding road to salvation and God was not finished molding her into the person he ultimately wanted her to become. This would come much later in life.

CHAPTER THREE

Sixteen Candles

For I know the thoughts that I think toward you,
says the Lord, thoughts of peace and not of evil,
to give you a future and a hope.

Then you will call upon me and go and pray to me, and I will listen to you.

Jeremiah 29:11-12

The year 1968 proved to be a milestone for Amelia (Amy) for on February 20, 1968 she turned a magical sixteen years old. Growing up there are a series of milestone years we all remember—ages 13, 16, 18 and 21 as each milestone marks a certain time in out life's development. After that we just count in multiples of ten (i.e. 30, 40, 50, 60, etc.).

George

In 1968 George was still living the American dream. He had quit his job at King Instruments and was working at TRW as a piston grinder. Before the end of the automotive age in America one could walk into a number of plants in the Greater Cleveland area and almost be guaranteed a high paying blue collar position. George was no different than any number of guys in his neighborhood. He kept his nose clean, punched a clock everyday, had an excellent work ethic, and provided well for his family. George's family was growing up right before his eyes. Amy was about to turn 16 and James was 14, George was 13, Annette was 8, and Kathy was 5. When Amy was turning 16 George was 37 and Joan was 35.

Things were looking well for the Sambula family. They lived in a great neighborhood and had made a lot of good friends. Amy was in her third year at Villa Angela. A new school had been built with open classrooms. The rest of the children all went to school at Our Lady of Perpetual Help and they all were doing very well in school at that time.

With George's new job and Joan working part-time at a local retailer (Uncle Bill's) they were living the American dream.

All was not well with America, however. Our country was involved in a war which seemed to divide the nation in two. George's own brother Jerome served in Vietnam along with a number of George's friends. George had prayed for his brother while he was in Vietnam where he was awarded a Purple Heart for injuries he received in this conflict.

Both of George's sons, James and George had long hair and this did not sit well with George. He didn't like the Hippie movement but he kind of left the boys alone and figured that they would have to learn on their own about life the hard way like he did.

George and the boys at the Two Crows were still hard at it in 1968. Just in case he didn't feel like going out with the boys, there was always plenty of beer and whiskey at home.

Amelia

Young love was still in the air for Amelia as she had just turned sixteen as fellow Clevelanders were shaking off the cold of another typically brutal winter and were eagerly awaiting the spring of 1968.

In 1964 Amy went to Euclid Beach Park on Little League Day and met her boyfriend Joey there. Joey was Amy's first boyfriend and they were still an item on Amy's 16th birthday. Beatlemania had swept America's teenagers and Joey and Amy were two more awe struck teens left in the wake of the Fab Four. On August 14, 1966 Amy and Joey went to the Beatles Concert at the Cleveland Municipal Stadium. They were two of 80,000 fans who paid $5.50 each to see the concert sponsored by Cleveland's number one rock-n-roll radio station, WIXY 1260. Amy and Joey were still an item when Amy turned sweet sixteen.

The world was rapidly changing for Amy and the rest of America in 1968. The Hippie movement was in full swing and Amy was OK with long hair. Both of her brothers had long hair. The Vietnam war touched Amy as her Uncle Jerome served in that war and received a Purple Heart. Amy and all the students at Villa Angela signed a long scroll supporting the troops and sent it to the Armed Forces serving in Southeast Asia.

The school year 1967-68 proved to continue to be an excellent time in Amy's life. She was surrounded by many classmates who truly loved her. Amy was very good at sports. She excelled in volleyball, softball, and basketball. She was also an excellent trumpet player. She was the only girl who participated in the St. Joe High School Band. St. Joe's was the all male equivalent to Villa Angela located in the same neighborhood as Amy's high school.

In the fall of 1968 Amy began her junior year at Villa Angela Academy which is an all girls school in Cleveland's Lakeshore neighborhood. Amy excelled in all subjects and was an excellent student. She was well liked by her fellow classmates and was a source of strength and companionship to a number of them. This can best be illustrated by the following birthday card that one of her classmates, Joni Morris, wrote to Amy and characterized Amy in the following manner:

- A devout worshiper
- A Christian
- A real Person
- A loyal friend
- A real buddy
- A counselor
- A guide
- A light
- A great person to know
- A carrier of love
- A spreader of Christ

Joni closed her hand-made birthday card with the following poem:

> A Poem About a Girl Named Amy:
>
> A girl I've known for quite a while,
> A girl with class and lots of style.
> A heart so huge it overflows with
> love for every girl & boy!!!
>
> She's cool, she's neat,
> And maybe you might call her sweet
> (but I don't know, It's up to you).
>
> She's know by many as
> Curly, Shirley (Temple) or Hot-lips Harry!
>
> I'm glad I know her,
> I'm glad I'm her friend.
> And this poem is coming to an end!!
>
>   Love
>   Luck
>   Laughs
>
>   Joni
>   Morris

Amy was viewed by her fellow classmates as a prayer partner and a pillar of strength as seen in the following letter written to Amy by one of her classmates, Patti:

> All I need is the Lord's peace, that's all. Pray that I find soon where I'm shutting Him out. He promised me He'd send His Peace. I believe that.
>
> Praise God! Take a peek at Roman's 8:29-36. That's my prayer at times like these.

> Listen, sweets—I have a feeling I am going to take an "R & R" (rest & relaxation) and come home this weekend. If I do, I'm sure I'll see you. If I don't—keep those Prayers comin'!!
>
> All my love & prayers
>
> Patti
> XOXO

Amy was not your typical rebellious teenager of the 1960's. She went to church with the family and went to prayer meetings at St. Joseph's and Villa Angela. George characterized Amy as very religious and said that she was very close to Jesus in her young walk as a Christian. It was evident that Amy had Jesus in her heart from her first year at Villa Angela. All her classmates knew that Amy had something special and that she was very close to Jesus. All the girls would ask her to pray for them about school and boyfriends and girlfriends and life in general as one travels into womanhood. All the girls knew that Amy was close to Jesus but did not know how close. Amy prayed for all the girls that talked to her or wrote to her. The girls just knew that she had the Holy Spirit in her heart and would all come to her and ask her to pray for them. Amy had given a series of talks at a Presbyterian Church in Euclid Ohio about her spirituality and how to find Christ. All the students were well aware of Amy's spiritual presence and that she indeed had something special about her. This is best evidenced by the following note she received from a classmate (Nancy Kovac) as they were entering their senior year in the fall of 1969:

> I can't believe were gonna be *Seniors* (hopefully)! Then going through college and work! Life certainly must be short! But, after all, we are just here for a "visit" and our *real* home awaits us. I only pray that my faith was *stronger*! I'm really so weak, Amy! Please pray for me, okay? Thanks! *Praise* the *Lord*!
>
> Love in Him
> Nancy (Kovac)
>
> P.S. Hope I see you soon!

Nancy had no idea how true her words would ring just a few short months later.

Carol Zimmerman

As Amy was turning sweet sixteen in February of 1968 Carol would be turning 24 two months later in April of 1968. Carol was still single and dating and had left her job at Huron Road hospital in 1968 to begin working at the larger Cleveland Clinic. Carol only worked at the clinic for six months because the Clinic was just too big for her. She had been used to a smaller neighborhood hospital and so she returned to Huron Road Hospital and stayed there until 1971 when she went to work for St. Luke's hospital.

Life changed for Carol in 1966 with the death of her father who succumbed to pancreatic cancer in June of 1966. Her father loved the holidays and all the festivities that went along with them. Christmas was never the same for Carol and to this day there is still sadness in her heart during the holidays.

Aside from the death of her father, life was good for Carol in 1968. She was still running out with her friends in the evenings and on the weekends and they all went dancing at Culps Shore Inn on Lakeshore Blvd, in Eastlake, Ohio on the weekends. Carol loved all rock-n-roll music and was especially fond of Elvis. No plans for marriage at that time. Carol was still going to Happy's a few times a week. She still drank beer, but really enjoyed her scotch.

Carol's church life was put on hold except for holidays, weddings, etc. Her weekends did not usually start until around 9:00 PM on Friday and Saturday nights and by the time Sunday AM service rolled around she just wanted to sleep in. Carol and her friends had one rule—don't call each other before 11:00 AM on either Saturday or Sunday morning.

Christ had not yet made an appearance into Carol's life at this point. Her mom would try and get Carol to watch Kathryn Kuhlman or Billy Graham on television but she absolutely had no interest in these television evangelists. She was too busy living in the world at that time.

Speaking of the world, by 1968 it was rapidly changing around Carol and the rest of America. Vietnam had a special impact on Carol's life. She had a cousin who served in Southeast Asia and she remembers that when he returned home from the war that he would turn off the radio or television when there was any mention of this conflict. He just could not stand to hear anything about Vietnam. He got into drinking and drugs over in Vietnam and he still struggles with alcohol to this day.

While Carol did not embrace the whole peace and love deal of the 1960's she had no issue with the hippie movement and long hair on men. She fondly recalls having a pair of platform shoes and how she almost killed herself walking in those things.

One area of the 1960's that Carol did embrace was drugs. Marijuana was her drug of choice and as Carol said—SHE LOVED POT. Carol also recalls (not fondly) her limited experimentation with acid. One time she was at the Indian Hills Apartments in Euclid, Ohio and she looked out the balcony doors and the cars were driving backwards on Euclid Avenue. Carol recalls that she did not know Jesus at that time but cried out to God to just let her be normal when she came off of her acid trip.

George and Joan, 1951.

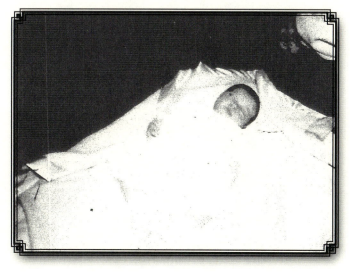

Amelia 3 1/2 weeks old, 1952.

George holding his Baby Girl Amelia, 1952.

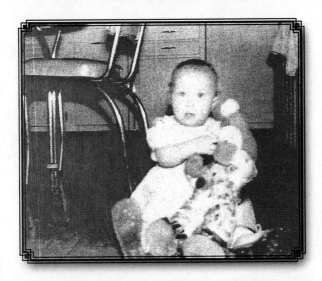

February 20, 1953
1st Birthday.

Amelia (Amy) 1st grade, 1959.

Amy, 7 yrs old.

Amelia with brothers Jim and George and sisters Annete and Kathleen, Nov. 1963.

Amelia with brother George and sisters Annette and Kathleen.

School Picture, 1967.

Amelia's Senior Picture, 1969.

CHAPTER FOUR

Calling All Angels

Then I looked, and I heard the voices of
many angels around the throne,
the living creatures, and the elders,
and the number of them was ten thousand times
ten thousand, and thousands of thousands,

saying with a loud voice:

"Worthy is the Lamb who was slain
To receive power and riches and wisdom,
And strength and honor and glory and blessing!"

Revelation 5:11-12

. . . . events that shredded people's lives and left them with gaping holes in the fabric of the day-to-day . . . .

from the book The Retribution by Val McDermid

There was a movie entitled "Pay it Forward" that was out a couple of years ago in which the young hero of the movie tragically lost his life in a senseless act of violence. As his parents stand there in disbelief the soundtrack plays the following song:

> "Calling all angels, Calling all angels
> Walk me thru this one
> Don't leave me alone . . . ."

As George and Joan were getting ready for bed the night of November 21, 1969 they had no idea how their world would be rocked in less than 24 hours. They had no idea that they would be calling on Heaven to provide for them an army of angels to help them get through their days one minute at a time—one step at a time—one foot in front of the other.

Often times as George and Joan had attended funerals for loved ones in the past and the priest or pastor or reverend would have quoted one or two of the following verses from the Bible:

> Yea, though I walk through the valley of
> the shadow of death, I will fear no evil;
> For you are with me;
> Your rod and Your staff they comfort me.
>
> Psalm 23:4

or

> "In My Father's house are many mansions;
> if it were not so, I would have told you.
> I go to prepare a place for you."
>
> "And if I go and prepare a place for you,
> I will come again and received you to Myself;
> that where I am, there you may be also.
>
> John 14:2, 3

or

> Therefore we are always confident,
> knowing that while we are at home in the body
> we are absent from the Lord.

For we walk by faith, not by sight.

We are confident, yes, well pleased
rather to be absent from the body
and to be present with the Lord.

2 Corinthians 5:6-8

George and Joan would offer their condolences and say how sorry they were and how they knew the grieved ones felt and would offer to do whatever they could to help provide relief at such times. At times such as these one often goes home and hugs their loved ones a little tighter and say praise to God that He had seen fit to spare them such grief.

George had no idea that in less than 24 hours his world would be rocked like it had never been rocked before and perhaps would never be rocked again. He had no idea that in less than 24 hours he would receive a right cross from the hand of God that he had no idea was coming. A punch from the heavens that would drop him to his knees. A punch that one day he would understand that had to be rendered to allow him to begin his path toward salvation.

CHAPTER FIVE

An Angel is Called Home—11.22.69

For yet a little while and the wicked
shall be no *more;*
Indeed, you will look diligently for his place,
But it *shall be* no *more.*

But the meek shall inherit the earth;
And shall delight themselves in the abundance of peace.

Psalm 37:10-11

And he was afraid and said,
"How awesome is this place!
This *is* none other than the house of God,
and this *is* the gate of Heaven."

Genesis 28:17

Then he said to Jesus, "Lord, remember me when you come into Your kingdom."
And Jesus said to him, "Assuredly, I say to you, today you will be with me in paradise."

Luke 23:42-43

Saturday started out like any other day in the Sambula household. As dusk turned to dark, however, the numbers 11.22.69 would be burned into the back of George's retinas for the rest of his natural days.

For those of us who are natives to Cleveland or Detroit or Buffalo or any other city on the shores of the Great Lakes we know that the month of November can be the precursor to the beginning of a long, cold and dark winter. While November is technically still fall, the days are shorter (thanks to the absence of daylight saving time), snow is often on the ground, and the winds from the Great Lakes produce what is known as lake effect snow, chilling all but the heartiest to the bone.

The weather forecast for November 22, 1969 called for no precipitation and a low of 32 and a high of 48. Almost a spring like day for most native Clevelanders. For one Clevelander in particular at approximately 6:30 PM the chilling affect of death would render her cold as she lay dead in a driveway literally steps from her home. For George and Joan their world would come to a crashing halt as they discovered that their very own Amelia (Amy) was this victim of a senseless crime. The logic of which could not be understood by anybody but God himself.

As George and his family were preparing for supper, James Sambula, age 15, thought he heard a gunshot and George thought that the noise sounded more like a car backfiring. So James went to the front porch at their home to see what he could see. From the white light of the streetlight he did see something—the figure of a young blonde girl wearing a brown coat with a dark brown collar and he recognized this person as his older sister Amelia.

George ran out of the house and ran to the vacant lot about ten feet west of their home and found his oldest daughter face down in the driveway about eight feet from the sidewalk. He grabbed her and hugged her and gave her a great big kiss and Amelia mouthed the words "oh, Dad" and George felt his daughter draw her last breath. He noticed a trail of blood running from the sidewalk to the body of his beloved child. Having failed to arouse his child, George fought back the tears and ran back to his house to tell his family what had happened. Joan quickly dialed 911 and called the Cleveland police.

Soon the area around the Pawnee home was filled with sirens as Cleveland's finest arrived on the scene from the 6th District police station a short distance from the Sambula home. As the police arrived, an ambulance arrived and transported Amelia to Euclid General Hospital, a two minute ride from the Sambula home. George and Joan immediately drove to this hospital where they were put in a waiting room. They waited between 2-4 hours and then a hospital staff member delivered the news. Their little girl was gone. They said that they could not revive Amy because there were five shots and two of the bullets struck vital organs. George and Joan had called friends to stay with the children when they went to the hospital. Upon hearing the news, George and Joan were beside themselves. They just held each other and cried and were numb. They could not believe that this was happening to them.

The two minute ride could have been two hours for time was not on the side of the medical staff at Euclid General. Amelia was pronounced dead upon her arrival at Euclid General.

Back at the Sambula home zone car officers were trying to get as much information as possible from George and Joan and their children to pass along to the Homicide Unit. This unit was headquartered at Police Headquarters at E. 21st and Payne Avenue, a foreboding fortress like structure which held the heartbeat of the men and women of the Cleveland Police Department.

The case was assigned to two underpaid and overworked Homicide Detectives, John Kaminsky and Harold Murphy, who jumped in their unmarked car and sped to the scene some ten miles from Police Headquarters. There is a current reality show on television called 48 Hours in which real world detectives attempt to solve homicides within the first 48 hours. Kaminsky and Murphy were well aware that the 48 hour clock began ticking at approximately 6:30 PM on November 22, 1969 and if they did not develop some leads as they headed to the crime scene at Pawnee Avenue N.E. off of E. 185th and Lakeshore Avenue their case would turn as cold as the November winds blowing off of Lake Erie.

As Kaminsky and Murphy rolled out of their unmarked police sedan they were met at the scene by a uniformed sergeant who offered little information. None of the neighbors saw anything and some said they heard shots, others said they thought they heard what sounded like firecrackers and others said they thought that they heard a car backfiring. One thing was for sure, Cleveland had one more homicide case to be solved in 1969 and Kaminsky and Murphy were given the task of trying to find the person responsible for this senseless slaying. The 48 hour clock was quickly clicking off to zero.

Kaminsky and Murphy began by turning their attention to the crime scene. They noted that Amelia had a short distance to walk from her part-time job at the Red Robin clothing store located at E. 185th Street to her home on Pawnee Avenue N.E. Probably no more than a 10 to 15 minute walk. The white light of the streetlights clearly showed a trail of blood from where Amelia was shot to where she crawled eight feet up the driveway of a neighbor's house located next to the home she shared with her mom and dad and her four siblings since she and her family moved there in 1963. The detectives believed that somebody had followed Amelia from E. 185th Street and caught up with her near her home and shot her a number of times.

The detectives had little to go on. No witnesses and no known motive. A quick canvas of the neighborhood revealed that Amelia was an honor student and the president of her class. She did not run with the wrong crowd and took pleasure in doing for others. Ever since she and her family moved to Cleveland in 1963, Amelia could be found spreading joy and happiness wherever she went. She was a model citizen and had no enemies and took pleasure in being a ray of sunshine to all she met. Nothing seemed to add up here. The rampant gang activity of today's urban centers had not yet begun to grow its roots. It was unheard of in 1969 to lose one's life just because you wore the red instead of blue or visa versa, or you were caught slinging crack on the wrong corner or just because. The most gang activity this quiet little neighborhood ever saw was a couple of Cleveland, Ohio Hell's Angels or a couple of African American Zulu motorcycle gang members riding their Harley Davidson bikes along scenic Lakeshore Avenue on a sunny Sunday afternoon. And the 48 hour clock was rapidly clicking down to zero at a point where the leads began to grow cold and memories began to fade.

Kaminsky and Murphy had little to go on at the moment. Their one sole lead centered around a local neighbor who reported that he had chased the killer but lost him a short time later. The detectives interviewed this individual, Robert Pustare, who told the detectives that he had witnessed the murder of Amelia and chased the perpetrator five or six blocks and almost caught him but lost him on a street called Arrowhead. Kaminsky and Murphy asked Pustare to retrace his steps for them and Pustare joined them in their unmarked car and showed them where he chased the perpetrator. At one point Pustare mentioned that he saw two young men in the parking lot of the supermarket and called to them to help him catch the perpetrator but they offered no assistance. Pustare described Amelia's killer as being six feet tall and on the husky side wearing a dark jacket. Kaminsky and Murphy then took the description back to the neighborhood and asked whether or not any of the neighbors saw anybody fitting this rather general description. No new leads were developed.

The two detectives then drove over to Euclid General Hospital to see if they could obtain any information from James Sambula or any of the other family members. Kaminsky and Murphy interviewed James at home who reported that he did not see anybody running from his sister's body as reported by Pustare. They then interviewed the doctor who attended to Amelia and learned that the victim was slain with a .38 caliber handgun and were able to obtain two slugs to be used for a future ballistics test.

Kaminsky and Murphy decided to refocus their attention on Pustare. They found it strange that the description of the killer Pustare had given them matched his own physical description—even to the color of jacket he was wearing. They decided to take Pustare back to headquarters and see what would develop. They were determined to beat that 48 hour clock.

At police headquarters Pustare appeared calm and eager to cooperate. Pustare again described the killer and the general description fit him. They talked with Pustare about his neighborhood walks on various side streets around the Pawnee neighborhood and the more they talked the more they liked Pustare as a fit for this crime. Kaminsky and Murphy took Pustare back to his home in the Pawnee neighborhood which the 28 year old Pustare shared with his mother and older sister. The detectives and Pustare later returned to police headquarters with five handguns that were found in the home of Pustare's mother. Pustare had stuck to his story and the detectives called it a day early Sunday morning with almost 20 hours ticking off of that 48 hour clock.

While the investigation was ongoing George went to the morgue to identify the body of his little girl. He then went to make funeral arrangements at Jacub's Funeral home on E. 185th. The priest who laid Amy to rest was Father Sommers. He was a personal friend of Amy and the family.

Day Two

On Sunday detectives Daniel McDonald and James Carbone arrived for work as Kaminsky and Murphy were clocking out. McDonald and Carbone agreed to follow up on the case and take on the 48 hour clock and again canvased the neighborhood and again talked with Pustare. Little else was produced in the way of evidence other than the fact that now all four detectives seemed to "like" Pustare as a possible fit for the crime.

Day Three

On Monday November 24, 1969 Thanksgiving week, Kaminsky and Murphy were back on the case. At the corner supermarket the two detectives were now able to interview the two stock boys who Pustare allegedly shouted to while pursuing Amelia's killer. Under questioning, both boys confirmed that they saw somebody matching Pustare's description running across the parking lot shouting that he went that way but that they only saw one man running and did not see anybody being pursued. Both boys also recalled that a car had pulled away from the parking lot just before the shots were fired on Saturday evening and that the car belonged to the son of a woman who worked at the supermarket.

Kaminsky and Murphy located the son of the woman and invited him to join them at headquarters on E.21st and Payne Avenue. After completing their interview, Kaminsky and Murphy learned that while this man was waiting on his mother he saw a young girl matching Amelia's description walk by followed by a tall husky man in a dark jacket fitting the general description of Robert Pustare.

A ballistics report from the crime lab found that one of the .38 caliber handguns taken from the home of Pustare's mother matched exactly the slugs taken from the victim and her clothing. The evidence gathered was enough to present their case to the prosecutor's office who agreed that justice was now served. The 48 hour clock had been stopped. Later that day the prosecutor's office filed first degree murder charges against Robert Pustare in the murder of Amelia (Amy) Sambula. He was indicted by a grand jury on December 1, 1969 for this senseless crime.

Day Five

As Robert Pustare awaited his trial in Cuyahoga County jail George and Joan buried their daughter on Wednesday November 26, 1969 one day before Thanksgiving. The six hundred classmates of Amelia's who lined both sides of Neff Avenue as Amelia's hearse passed by were little comfort to George and Joan and their family as their lives were changed forever. George recalled that he and his wife were in tears the whole time going through the funeral. George recalls being numb. Amy was buried at All Souls Cemetery on Rt. 6 in Chardon, Ohio. George recalls that they had people coming to the house from all over—the news media, television and even Senator Vanik came to the house to pay his respects. All that time George and Joan just wanted to be left alone. God was not finished molding the man he wanted George to become—in fact the long and winding road that God had planned for George had just begun.

Author's Note: Each of the four Sambula children were asked if they would like to share their thoughts as to what they were feeling relative to the tragic events of 11.22.69. Three of the siblings, George and James and Kathy elected not to offer a glimpse of their thoughts on that day and their wishes have certainly been respected. Amy's sister, Annette, who was eight at the time of this tragedy had the following insight.

Annette

Annette recalls coming in from playing outside and being told to wash up because they were going to eat dinner. She recalls that while her mom was in the kitchen cooking dinner, she and her siblings were sitting in front of the television set in the living room watching the news and waiting for dinner to be served. Annette said that she and her family heard what they thought was a car backfiring. She recalled her older brother Jim running out first to see what was up because they were all waiting for Amelia to come home for supper and to be walking in the door any minute. She heard Jim scream "oh my God, Amelia had been shot." Annette could not recall where her parents were at that time, but she believes that at that point her mom had run outside and was calling for more blankets to keep Amelia warm. Annette recalls going outside and following her older brother Jim and may have been leaning over the porch railing viewing what was going on at that time. She believed that her dad George was calling 911 or the police for an ambulance but that the dispatcher on the other end of the phone line seemed to be in disbelief and that her dad was very upset because he had to call a second or third time since no vehicle showed up at the scene. Annette recalled the neighbor across the street coming to watch her younger sister Kathy and her while her parents went to the hospital with Amelia. Annette also recalled to this day the horrified look on her mom's face as she walked up their front steps as her dad was trying to hold her up since she appeared to not be able to walk on her own. Annette finally painfully recalled her mom telling them that Amelia was gone and then her mom collapsed as if she was a rag doll.

CHAPTER SIX

Innocent Blood

And because of the innocent blood that he had shed; for he had filled Jerusalem with innocent blood, which the Lord would not pardon

2 Kings 24:4

For I, the Lord, love justice.

Isaiah 61:8

Let the heavens declare his righteousness,
For God Himself is judge.

Psalm 50:6

While Robert Pustare was awaiting trial for murder in case number 94219 in the matter of the of Ohio V. Robert Pustare, which was to be heard in the Common Pleas section of the criminal court in the courtroom of Judge Joseph J. Nahra, his attorneys, S.A. Terrell and Martin A. Rini, set in motion a series of salvos aimed on derailing the prosecutor's case in this matter. On January 8, 1970 they filed the following motion:

Now comes Robert Pustare and his attorneys, Seymour A. Terrell and Martin A. Rini and moves this honorable court for an order requesting that the prosecuting attorney and the Police Department of the city of Cleveland submit the gun held in evidence in this matter to David Cowels, an independent ballistics expert for examination of the gun and the bullets which will be fired from the gun during the test.

The evidence in the above captioned case will depend largely upon ballistics tests of a gun in the possession of the Cleveland Police Department. The defendant hereby requests that David Cowels, an independent ballistics expert, be given the opportunity to make an examination of the said weapon and to make firing tests and then examine the marking on the spent bullets.

Attorneys Terrell and Rini then filed the following motion with the court:

Now comes the defendant, Robert Pustare, by his attorneys, Seymour A. Terrell and Martin Rini, and moves this honorable court for an order requiring the County Prosecutor to grant the following information to the said defendant so that he may be in a better position to answer the indictment of first degree murder.

1. How did the defendant kill the victim, Amelia Sambula?

2. In what respect did the defendant unlawfully, purposely and of deliberate and premeditated malice kill Amelia Sambula?

3. What was the time of day and the location of the alleged homicide?

4. What type of weapon was used to kill said victim, and was this weapon the one that caused her death and if so, in what manner did she die.

On June 24, 1970 the prosecution presented the following bill of particulars with the court outlining the case against the defendant and answering the above motion filed by Attorneys Seymour and Rini.

Bill of Particulars

The People incorporate herein all of the allegations of the indictment and further state that Robert Pustare on or about the 22nd day of November, 1969, at the County of Cuyahoga, unlawfully, and of deliberate and premeditated malice killed Amelia Sambula.

Said victim, Amelia Sambula, was murdered in front of the home located at 18717 Pawnee Avenue, in the City of Cleveland, County of Cuyahoga, State of Ohio, at or about the hours of 6:00 PM to 7:00 PM, when the defendant, Robert Pustare, while armed with a .38 caliber Smith & Wesson gun did unlawfully, purposely and of deliberate and premeditated malice shoot the victim multiple times about her body causing the death of the victim as a result of multiple wounds of the chest with perforations of the heart and lungs.

A copy of the coroner's report of autopsy Case No. 134501, Autopsy No. M-30223 is attached hereto and made a part hereof.

The prosecuting attorney says the other matters requested in the Motion for a Bill of Particulars are evidence which is proof of the facts in the indictment and will be introduced at the time of the trial of this case.

Prior to the start of the trial Robert Pustare's Attorneys, S. A. Terrell and Martin A. Rini, entered a plea of not guilty to the indictment and not guilty by reason of insanity. Attorneys Terrell and Rini argued that the defendants Miranda rights were violated as follows:

Any claim by the prosecutor that this Defendant gave the police his consent that they could go into his house and secure the weapons there is ineffective, if any such consent was given after defendant had requested at attorney and such request had been denied. The continued questioning by the police violated the mandates of criminal procedure as set out in the *Miranda* decision and this defendant's privilege against self-incrimination was also disregarded by such continued questioning. This motion was filed on May 28, 1970.

On June 12, 1970 fifty subpoenas were sent to perspective members of the jury and on June 20, 1970 subpoenas were sent to fifteen witnesses including six members of the Cleveland Police Department. The trial was set for July 6, 1970.

By July 16, 1970 both sides had rested their case and the following journal entry was made in the court record:

This day again came the Prosecuting Attorney on behalf of the State, and defendant Robert Pustare was brought into court in custody of the sheriff; his counsel coming; also came the jury, duly impaneled and sworn, and the trial proceeded.

And the said jury having heard all the testimony adduced, the arguments of counsel, and the Charge of the Court, alternate jurors dismissed, retired to their room for deliberation.

After two days of deliberation a second journal entry was made into the court record on July 18, 1970. This entry read as follows:

This day again comes the Prosecuting Attorney on behalf of the State and defendant Robert Pustare was brought into court, his counsel also coming, and the Jury duly impaneled and sworn and they retired to their room in charge of the bailiff, for further deliberation.

Now comes the jury, conducted into court by the bailiff and return the following verdict in writing to-wit: "We, the Jury in this case, being duly impaneled and sworn, do find the defendant Robert Pustare guilty of Murder in the first degree RC 2901.01 as charged in the indictment, and we do further recommend Mercy."

Whereupon, the Court informed the defendant of the verdict of the Jury and inquired of him if he had anything to say why judgment should not be pronounced against him and he having nothing but what he hath already said:

It is therefore ordered and adjudged by the Court the defendant Robert Pustare be imprisoned and confined in the Ohio State Penitentiary, Columbus, Ohio, for an undetermined period, according to law, and that he pay the costs of prosecution, for which execution is hereby awarded.

On August 1, 1970 Robert Pustare's Attorney Martin A. Rini appealed the verdict to the Court of Appeals Eight District Circuit. This appeal was denied. While in prison Robert Pustare unsuccessfully appealed his conviction on two occasions.

On January 19 1988, Robert Pustare was released from prison. The Sambula family was never notified of this fact. They were later notified by their friend, a police detective.

CHAPTER SEVEN

Calling Hours 2 to 4 and 7 to 9

So when this corruptible has put on
incorruption, and this mortal has put on
immortality, then shall be brought to pass
the saying that is written: *Death is
swallowed up in victory,"*

*"O Death, where is your sting?
O Hades where is your victory?"*

The sting of death is sin, and the strength
of sin is the law.

But thanks to God, who gives us the
victory through our Lord Jesus Christ

Therefore, my beloved brethren, be steadfast,
immovable, always abounding in the work
of the Lord, knowing that your labor is not
in vain in the Lord.

I Corinthians
15:54-58

Funerals can be a strange place to be for both the living and the dead. I have personally attended what my former Pastor used to call "hope so" and "know so" funerals. As a Protestant, my former Pastor would label the Catholic funerals as "hope so" with the participants hoping that their loved ones would have done enough good works to get them into heaven. Pastor Murphey would contrast this with that of the Protestant funeral in which the deceased had already invited Christ into his or her heart and was assured a place in heaven.

When writing this book the publisher sent me a first galley draft that Carol and George and I had to review. In reviewing this chapter all of us felt that a re-work was in order when it came to "labeling" one religion over another in terms of who gets into heaven and who does not.

While sitting in church on the 16th of February 2013, I was thinking about how to re-work this chapter while listening to Pastor Majetich's sermon. Pastor was giving a sermon on "Being Counted as Worthy" and he directed the congregation to 1 Thessalonians 2:12. This passage states "that you would have a walk worthy of God who calls you into His own kingdom and glory." After hearing this verse, I knew that I had a God given answer to the dilemma that George and Carol and I had been dealing with at the time of the first proof. The point here, and message that God conveyed to me in February, is that our future destiny is not determined by what religion we practice but whether we have a relationship with Jesus Christ. This relationship with Christ and how this is linked to our salvation can been seen in the following text from I John 5:11-13 which reads as follows: "And this is the testimony that God has given us eternal life, and this life is His Son. He who has the Son has life: he who does not have the Son does not have life. These things I have written to you who believe in the name of the Son of God, that you may know that you have eternal life, and that you may continue to believe in the name of the Son of God."

Paul tells us in Romans 10:9 "that if you confess with your mouth the Lord Jesus and believe in your heart that God has raised Him from the dead, you will be saved." Whatever religious nameplate we wear here on earth has nothing to do with our admission into a heavenly home. Albeit Catholic or Protestant or Jew or Muslim our relationship with Jesus Christ will be our ticket to glory and not where we spent our Saturday or Sunday mornings.

As memory serves me Catholics seem to have the market cornered on mourning with three full days of a wake with calling hours between 2 to

4 and 7 to 9 for three days before the burial. It is against this backdrop that George and Joan laid their Amelia to rest on November 26, 1969. Whether or not the Sambulas were Catholic or not was not the issue here. Given the fact that their Amelia had a saving knowledge of Jesus Christ as her Lord and Savior, both George and Joan could also be assured that should they have the same relationship one day they and their daughter would be reunited again. History tells us that in 1969 George Sambula had not yet fallen to his knees, admitted he was a sinner, and invited Jesus Christ into his heart. God was not yet through with George in terms of molding George into the man God wanted him to become. George would have to go through additional life changing trials and tribulations before such a transformation would take place. The death of his beloved daughter Amelia was one in a series of events in his life that George needed to pass through to have him get to where God wanted him to go. The journey was not yet over and had actually just begun in the winter of 1969.

CHAPTER EIGHT

Home for the Holidays

All the inhabitant of the earth are reputed as nothing.
He does according to His will in the army of heaven
And among the inhabitants of the earth.

No one can restrain His hand or say to him,
"What have You done?"

Daniel 4:35

Christmas 1969 was extremely painful for the Sambula family. George recalls that it was a very sad time but the family did all the things anyone does at that time. They carried on as anyone does at Christmas. They had a real Christmas tree and exchanged presents and had a Christmas dinner. The family went to midnight mass and early service on Christmas. George knew in his heart of hearts that life as they knew it would never be the same. The death of Amy took a lot of joy out of his family. All of their hearts were broken from the grief. People from Amy's school and George's church would come by and try and fill the void in their lives. There was nothing anybody could really do or say to replace this void.

The shortest verse in the Bible is "Jesus wept". This refers to our Savior's reaction to the death of his friend, Lazarus. Although Jesus knew that he would raise his friend up from the dead, the human side of Jesus still grieved.

As Christians we understand that time is fleeting and life is precious and that for those of us who are "born again" and have invited Christ into our lives we have blessed assurance that we will be reunited in glory with our loves ones again and forever. George did not have this blessed assurance in 1969.

What George did have was his drinking to drown his sorrows and he took to that salvation with a vengeance. George was a drinker before this tragedy and tried to control his drinking before the untimely death of Amy. George recalls that at that time he had lost control of his drinking and just wanted to drown his sorrow. George would later come to find that the two detectives assigned to his daughter's case, Kaminsky and Murphy, visited the Two Crows and found out that Amy's murderer visited the very same bar after her murder as George visited.

In helping me to write this book George and Carol provided me with a number of Amy's treasures that pointed to who she was and what she believed. George and Carol shared with me the following bookmark which reads as follows:

> NOT TILL THE LOOM IS SILENT
> AND THE SHUTTLES CEASE TO FLY,
> SHALL GOD UNROLL THE CANVAS AND EXPLAIN
> WHY THE DARK THREADS ARE AS NEEDFUL,
> IN THE WEAVER'S SKILLFUL HAND,
> AS THE THREADS OF GOLD AND SILVER
> IN THE PATTERN HE HAS PLANNED.

As George's story unfolds on these pages we will all discover that one day George (like so many of us) will come to appreciate the dark threads as well as the threads of silver and gold. Only then will he be released from the shadow of Amy's death.

CHAPTER NINE

Players To Be Named Later

From the place of His habitation He looks
On all the inhabitants of the earth;
He fashions their hearts individually;
He considers all their works.

Psalm 33:14-15

Carol Zimmerman

In Sunday's Plain Dealer on November 23, 1969 an article appeared with the headlines 'Model Girl', 17, Slain Near Sidewalk Near Home. This article went on to say that a 17 year-old girl, an honor student at Villa Angela Academy, was shot and stabbed to death last night 100 feet from her home at 18715 Pawnee Avenue N.E. The article stated that the victim was Amelia Theresa Sambula who the nuns at the all girls school described as a "model pupil and a real saint." The article went on to say that the police had made an arrest but that they could find no motive for the slaying. According to the article Amelia's father, George Sambula, described her as a "deeply religious, happy girl" who "always wanted to spread her religion and help other people." The article went on to say that Father Kenneth Sommers, Chaplin at St. Joseph High School had just taken Amelia to address a youth group in Youngstown last Sunday and that "religion meant everything to her."

It is quite possible that on Sunday November 23, 1969 Carol could have very well picked up her Sunday edition of the Plain Dealer and read this very same article. Carol could have paused and thought how sad these turn of events were for the family and would go on with her day. She had no idea what role God had outlined for her in the further development of this story as well as the further development of George's walk as a Christian. Future lessons were planned for both Carol and her future husband, George, on grace and faith and salvation and God's divine plan for us all.

Author, Author

Between reading the sport page and scanning the classified for hot rod auto parts it is quite possible that the author at age 18 (one year older than Amelia) could have very well read this article during his Sunday morning trek through the Plain Dealer. The author too could have paused for a minute and reflected on this sad moment for the Sambula family and gone about his day. He would have no idea that before the beginning of time God knew that one day the author would meet George and Carol Sambula and be given the honor of putting God's grace and mercy and George and Carol's faith lessons on paper for all to read—to serve as hope for the hopeless and faith for the faithless.

CHAPTER TEN

Our Father Who Art in Heaven

"In this manner, therefore pray:

Our Father in heaven,
Hallowed be your name.
Your kingdom come.
Your will be done
On earth as it is in heaven.
Give us this day our daily bread.
And forgive us our debts,
As we forgive our debtors.
And do not lead us into temptation,
But deliver us from the evil one.

Matthew 6:9-12

On December 9, 1969 George and Joan Sambula received the following letter from St Mary's College in Norte Dame, Indiana:

December 9, 1969

Mr. and Mrs. Sambula
18715 Pawnee Avenue
Cleveland, Ohio 44119

Dear Mr. and Mrs. Sambula:

Today I received from Sister Mary Afra the clippings concerning Amelia's death. God's ways are strange. The closing lines of Amelia's autobiography are strangely prophetic. Since she may not have kept a copy of what she wrote on her application form, I am returning one of the two copies for you to have. It does seem as if God had accepted the offering of her life. We shall not know until eternity the full effect of her life and death on others.

The Mass of December 8th was said for her and you by Father John Cavanough our chaplain. Be assured that the Sisters here will keep you in prayerful remembrance.

Sincerely Yours,

Sister M. Raphaelita, C.S.C.
Director of Admissions

Amy's application to Norte Dame College, which was completed on October 6, 1969 stated (in part) the following:

Through a beautiful nun I not only began to understand myself and grow but also make a better and more genuine commitment to Christ....

I am excited and hopeful for my future. I am thankful to my parents for their love has helped me to be what I am. I love and believe in people and hope I can serve them in my life's work and offer all that my life is to God.

As mentioned earlier God called Amy to be by His side 46 days after this application was written. While we can't at times understand why God does what he does, we all can rest in the blessed assurance that He does not make mistakes and that our lives (as frail as they are) are in His hands from our first breath to our last.

CHAPTER ELEVEN

See You on the Other Side

Jesus said to her, "I am the resurrection and the life.
He who believes in Me, though he may die, He shall live.

"And whoever lives and believes in Me shall never
die. Do you believe this?"

John 11:25-26

"For so the Lord has commanded us:

I have set you to be a
light to the Gentiles.
That you should be for salvation
to the ends of the earth."

Acts 13:47

On December 11, 1969 George and Joan received another letter pointing to the good work that Amy had begun during her time her on earth. The letter reads as follows:

December 11, 1969

Mr. and Mrs. Sambula
18715 Pawnee
Euclid, Ohio

Dear Mr. and Mrs. Sambula:

We wanted you to know how much Amy's testimony meant to us here at Wickliffe United Presbyterian Church. We were privileged to have her speak at our Bible Classes in January 1969, and again only a few weeks ago. She shared with us her personal relationship with her Creator—God—Christ—and the Holy Spirit. How if you could only accept Christ as the saving force in your live—it could open to you a whole new way of looking on life—God's way.

He certainly must have her with Him now—a certain amount of her conviction rubbed off on some of us here—quite a legacy for a 17-year-old!

We all wanted you to know we are praying with you, and hope God's comfort will be with you now, and in the days ahead.

(This letter was signed by 25 members of the Bible Class).

Again, we do not know God's will for each of us. We do know that He has a plan for us and that part of this plan includes inviting his Son into our hearts. Perhaps God's entire plan for Amy was to have her address this Bible Class twice in 1969 to bring perhaps one or two students to Christ—and with this completed her work here on earth.

Amy created this during her senior year.
It was quite evident she had Christ in her heart at that time.

CHAPTER TWELVE

One Year Later

For His anger is but for a moment, His favor is for life;
Weeping may endure for a night, But joy comes in the morning

Psalm 30:5

You have turned for me my mourning into dancing

Psalm 30:11

"Come to Me, all you who labor and are heavy Laden,
and I will give you rest.
"Take My yoke upon you and learn from Me,
for I am gentle and lowly in heart, and you
will find rest for your souls.
"For my yoke is easy and My burden is light."

Matthew 11:28-30

I can't even begin to imagine what November 22, 1970 must have been like for George and Joan as they approached the one year anniversary of their daughter's murder. God seems to have a unique way of working things out as we walk on this earth playing the game of life. George Sambula is one of several parents who have lost children who are members of our small country church in Newbury, Ohio. Dick and Faith Whitcomb lost their son Rick to murder 15 years ago. Val Rasch's son Mark Allen had succumbed to an illness in 2006. Bruce and Marcia Reilly lost their son Shawn to an automobile accident three years ago. I was not present to witness the grief of each of these parents as the one year anniversary of the deaths of their children came and went. I was present, however, on February 5, 2011 when two of our church members, David and Tammy Wilkes, invited a number of us to a graveside memorial for their son, Shawn, who was killed in an automobile accident on February 5, 2010. Their grief was almost too much to bear. Despite the fact that both Tammy and David were assured that their son was in heaven, this realization did little to sooth the rawness of that cold February afternoon as they searched in vain for words of comfort. Tammy read a prepared statement that she had written at the time of Shawn's death but could not find the strength to deliver her words until one year later. David's cheeks were tear stained as all he could muster was let's count to three and shout out a "Hey, Shawn" as the memorial service ended.

George did share with me that at the mark of the one year anniversary of Amy's death a $500.00 donation kicked off a scholarship foundation in loving memory of his daughter. As a special tribute to Amy the school band played the song Impossible Dream which Amy had played so often for George on her trumpet. May the following words to this song help Tammy and David and others find comfort as they have comforted George throughout the years:

Impossible Dream

> To dream the impossible dream
> To fight the unbeatable foe
> To bear the unbearable sorrow
> To run where the brave dare not go
> To right the unrightable wrong
> To love, pure and chaste from afar
> To try, when your arms are too weary
> To reach the unreachable star.
>
> This is my quest: to follow that star
> No matter how hopeless, no matter how far
> To be willing to give, without question or pause
> To be willing to march into hell for a heavenly cause

And I know if I'll only be true to this glorious quest
That my heart will lie peaceful and calm
When I'm laid to my rest.

And the world will be better for this
That one man, scorned and covered with scars,
Still strove with his last ounce of courage
To reach the unreachable star.

May all who read this book and are heavy laden with the trouble of the world come to understand that our Lord and Savior stands ready to help you lift the yoke of the world off of your shoulders.

This is a bookmark that was Amy's. She liked it so much she entered it in a journal of special writings she wrote for school.

CHAPTER THIRTEEN

Lightning Strikes Again—09.17.75

For you have need of endurance, so that after you have done the will of God, you may receive the promise

Hebrews 10:36

Therefore what God has joined together, let not man separate.

Mark 10:9

God has promised us that he will never give us more trouble than we could handle. George was not sure of this promise when he buried his wife Joan on September 17, 1975. Joan started with a severe cough that would not quit. Within a matter of two to three months Joan was called home to be with the Lord. She was never diagnosed with cancer until after her death. Joan had five specialists who were unable to diagnose her case. Joan sensed that she was in trouble when the coughing continued and there was nothing that could be done for her. George and Joan talked about her condition a lot and Joan was really afraid for her future. Her condition was quite baffling because she never smoked nor drank. It was hard for George to see his wife in that condition. He has wished that he had this condition instead of Joan—but God had other plans.

Joan died on September 17, 1975 at Euclid General Hospital which was the same hospital Amy was taken to almost six years earlier. Joan's funeral was held at the same Church as Amy's, Our Lady of Perpetual Help, and Joan was laid to rest at All Souls Cemetery next to their daughter Amy. At the time of Joan's death their two oldest sons, Jim and George, were already out of the house. Jim was a manager at a Bi-Rite food store and George had a pizza shop on E. 185th Street near the family residence. Fifteen year old Annette and twelve year old Kathy were still at home and George was left with no choice but to pick up the pieces and take care of the rest of his family. Often times George would either drink or cry himself to sleep at night but the next morning he got the girls off to school and he went to work. As many times as George wanted to just go to sleep and never get up he still took his role as father and provider very seriously and continued to care for his remaining loved ones while clinging to the memory of Amy and now Joan.

George recalls that in his wildest dreams he would never imagine that he would lose his wife so close to having lost his daughter. He had done a lot of praying at this point in his life and asked God to restore Joan's health but this was not meant to be. If you would have asked George in 1968 if he would have ever been able to bury both his oldest child and his wife he would have said no and laughed out loud. He never would have even imagined that he would have been able to bear the pain and anguish that he would soon face. But before the sands of time God knew what George would have to endure to eventually become the man that God wanted him to become. Every tear that George shed was held in God's mighty hand as a source for future comfort and nurturing.

CHAPTER FOURTEEN

George and AA

"As we see life as a pilgrimage between two moments of nakedness"

From John Stott's book The Radical Disciple

"as so it may not happen, when he hears the words of this curse, that he blesses himself in his heart, saying 'I shall have peace, enough though I walk in the imagination of my heart'—and though the drunkard could be included with the sober."

Deuteronomy 29:19

"Have I not commanded you? Be strong and of good courage: do not be afraid nor be dismayed, for the Lord your God is with you wherever you go."

Joshua 1:9

Alcohol and George became even better friends after the death of Amy and then his wife Joan. The pain of losing two loves ones with the span of a few months short of six years was more than George could bear. Amy's loss in 1969 coupled with Joan's loss in 1975 just drove George to the brink of destruction. His only escape was alcohol and he turned to this "friend" more than ever after September of 1975.

No matter how much the alcohol abuse affected George's health he just could not seem to fight this addiction. The emotional pain that the alcohol numbed seemed to be worth the physical pain that the addiction had been causing.

George was a daily drinker who drank before work, at work and after work at the Two Crows. He could count on one hand the number of times he went out to lunch and did not drink. Alcohol controlled every waking moment of his life. All he could think about was that next drink—that next pain killing drink into which he could drown his sorrows.

It is not that George did not love the rest of his children—he loved them very much. If it was not for his remaining children George would not be here today. Although George understood that he had to take care of his children and that he had to keep his job and put food on the table and a roof over their heads the alcohol and its mind numbing effects came first. The hurt and pain of losing both his daughter and his wife was almost unbearable and for those fleeting moments the alcohol seemed to lessen this pain.

The progression of George's drinking seemed to have little impact on the remaining children. George believes that by that time in his life his drinking was just a normal part of his life and their lives as well. George always had beer and whiskey at home to drink. The children saw George's drinking both before and after the loss of Amy and Joan and by now that was just part of all of their lives.

George would like to say that he stopped drinking for the children but that was not the case. They never asked him to stop and he never thought that it was a problem for them—it was a physical problem for him.

The drinking progressed rapidly after Joan's death in 1975 and the drinking made George increasingly ill. All this drinking was catching up with him and he knew that he had to do something. He became sick and tired of being sick and tired.

George admits that if the drinking had not made him sick he never would have stopped drinking. He says that it was the amount of drinking that he did that caught up with him. George recalls that in his early days at the Two Crows that he was a controlled drinker. Just throw back a couple with the boys and call it a night. George's troubles with alcohol began when he tried to fill the void left by the loss of Amy and Joan with alcohol. No matter how much he had spiraled out of control the pain would not subside. No matter how much he drank that pain in his heart did not go away and now this drinking was affecting him physically.

In 1977 and 1978 George tried to stop cold turkey on his own and this did not work. His alcohol abuse caused him to be hospitalized three times at Euclid General Hospital and he was given his last rites on each occasion.

George recalled the first time he tried to quit drinking he tried cold turkey and about the third day or so he went into a convulsion and ended up at Euclid General. During his stay at the hospital he was asleep and saw a bright light as he was going into a tunnel. When he got to the other side of the tunnel he felt like he was in paradise. He felt like he was in another dimension and that the Lord Jesus Christ came to bring him back to life on earth.

On another occasion George was again in the hospital and again he felt his soul leave his body. He saw three figures clothed in black. They had hoods on their heads and their hoods came to a point. Their faces were blotted out and covered with the blackness.

When George was hospitalized a third time he again had an out of body experience. On this occasion his whole life flashed before him in a split second. George said that it happened so fast and that everything he had ever done was right there before his very eyes. He said that he heard a language that he never heard spoken before—yet he understood every word that he heard.

George has three dates burned in his memory bank that will never leave him.
One, on November 22, 1969 the Lord called Amy home. Two, on September 17, 1975 the Lord called Joan to his side. Three, on January 24, 1978 George defeated alcoholism.

On January 24, 1978 George admitted himself into Rosemary Hall for treatment for his addiction which had been controlling his life for far too long. George had now gotten professional help for the treatment of his disease. He was taken off of alcohol slowly with the proper medication. He was given a list of chores to do such as making your own bed and helping with general chores. George said that when he went to Rosemary Hall he knew that he had taken his last drink. He had bottomed out and hit rock bottom. He was tired of being a drunk and ruining his life and the lives of his loved ones. George had wanted to stop drinking and had made a choice to turn his life around. He had no where else to go but up from this point on.

Coupled with his treatment for the physical side of his addiction George also was introduced to Alcohol Anonymous which provided him with help in dealing with the emotional side of his addiction. Coming out of Rosemary Hall George attended his first AA meeting and announced "Hi, my name is George and I am an alcoholic." George can still recall how good that felt to admit that he had an addiction and that he was taking the steps necessary to rid himself of this evil.

George went to AA meetings at least once a day and sometimes two and three times a day and proudly wore his badge of courage and announced "Hi, my name is George and I am an alcoholic." He kept going to daily meetings and after two years became the President of the AA Humble Group for the next four years. George then became President of the Catholic Calix Society at Rosemary Hall. He also served as an officer at the downtown AA Central Office for three years.

During George's time in AA he sponsored about ten fellow addicts. Some of these alcoholics would find sobriety right away and some would stay sober and some would not. For some it would take years to remain clean and sober. George believed that God had a special place for him in AA—not just as a sponsor but as a friend to those who just needed to talk to somebody.

George recalls that none of his drinking buddies from the Two Crows ever came to ask him to help them stop drinking. All of the people that he helped were referrals from the AA Central Office or an AA meeting. After George defeated alcoholism he had stopped into the Two Crows on several occasions but was never tempted to have a drink again. He has even served alcohol at a function or two and was never tempted. He says that the temptation has left him completely.

George credits his life of sobriety with his relationship with Jesus Christ—but that story is yet to come later on in this book.

CHAPTER FIFTEEN

Carol and AA

And he who reaps receives wages and gathers fruit for eternal life, that both he who sows and reaps may rejoice together."

John 4:36

"Most assuredly, I say to you, he who believes in Me has everlasting life."

John 6:47

No temptation has overtaken you except such as is common to man; but God is faithful, who will not allow you to be tempted beyond what you are able, but with temptation will also make the way of escape, that you may be able to bear it.

I Corinthians 10:13

They say that God moves in mysterious ways. I am not sure who "they" are—but whoever they are they really do not know God. God's ways are mysterious for those of us who know and love him. He has a plan for each and every one of us and as George was going through the living hell of dealing with the death of his daughter in 1969 and death of his wife Joan in 1976, Carol was going through a living hell of her own as we shall see in a minute. When I asked Carol to tell me about her experience with AA she lovingly reminded me that while she had no reluctance in telling me her story that this book was really about Amy. While I agree with Carol that this book is about Amy it is also about God and how He melded and molded the lives of Carol and George into one. How he took them down separate paths and introduced them to their separate versions of living hell only to have them come out of their separate experiences stronger, more complete, and as His loving children having invited Christ into their hearts. Here is Carol's story of her AA experience . . . .

Carol said that her heaviest drinking occurred between the ages of 27 to 32. She recalled that at that time she worked at a local hospital and she would meet her friends at Happy's or at the Noble Inn after work. While each venue attracted a different crowd all of Carol's drinking buddies were single and all about the same age, in their twenties. Carol and her friends had good jobs and went to work daily and just wanted to go out and have fun. She recalled that every day was a good time and they just loved having fun together. Carol said that it was like rewarding yourself after a long day at work.

According to Carol she never dreamed of drinking at work—not because she did not want a drink but that she knew that she could not stop with just one drink. Carol admits that she was clearly an alcoholic. Carol said that one drink was never enough and that if she was in a situation in which she could have just one drink she would pass—because she knew that she could not stop with just one drink. She knew that she was addicted to alcohol and that stopping with one drink would not help her tackle her addiction.

Carol freely admitted that she drove and drank often during her career as an alcoholic. She recalls one time when it was dark and raining one night and she had been at Happy's and left to go home for the evening. Carol made a left turn on Lakeshore Boulevard and didn't see a person crossing the street and missed hitting the person by about an inch. She had never forgotten that night and how close she came taking somebody's life as a result of her addiction.

Carol and her family never discussed her drinking. She recalled that in her drinking days that when the family got together there was always drinking among the adults. When Carol and her cousins got older they engaged in the family drinking ritual. Carol and her cousins lived in different parts of the country and when they got together they liked to have a good time together. She did not characterize herself and her family as under the bridge drunks—just people who like to have fun.

While Carol did not classify herself as a falling down drunk she freely admitted that when she would leave Happy's or the Noble Inn she would come home and have a few more drinks before she went to bed. Carol said that drink craved drink and she always wanted just one more.

Unlike George, Carol was never hospitalized for her addiction. She admits that she would have liked to quit but she always found herself going out for that drink after work and then was unable so stop once she started. The weekends were big drinking times for Carol and her friends. She would normally stay home and chill out on Sundays. She could stop drinking for that one day and found that she was craving a drink again when Monday rolled around. All of the parties and picnics that she attended included alcohol and at times a little pot. This was just the life that Carol had lived and had no idea how to stop the madness. The days and nights were just one alcoholic blur as Carol rolled down the highway of life.

Things changed dramatically for Carol in the summer of 1976 when she lost her mother. While George found sobriety first and Christ later—for Carol the opposite was true. On July 12, 1976 Carol fell to her knees and admitted that she was a sinner and invited Jesus Christ into her heart. From that time forward Carol's life has never been the same.

On August 24, 1976 the Holy Spirit led Carol to call the AA Central Office to inquire about attending an AA meeting. Carol thought that she would perhaps go to a meeting once in a while but she would not to give up her friends. Jesus, however, had other plans for Carol.

Carol went to her first meeting on that hot summer night in August and was introduced to her sponsor, Ann Lorenzo. At first Carol was apprehensive but Ann encouraged her.

Carol went to her first meeting at a church just up the road from Happy's (talk about divine intervention) and said "Hi, my name is Carol and I am an alcoholic." At this first meeting she met Ann Lorenzo, a lady who would volunteer to be her sponsor. Carol asked how often she should go to meetings and Ann told her that if she drank everyday then she should go to a meeting every day. Just imagine how many times Carol passed that church which held the AA meeting never dreaming that one day this would be the place where she would start her sobriety.

The first couple of weeks were very hard for Carol. Twice during these first two weeks Carol and her friends went to Happy's and Carol just stayed in her car and sat in the parking lot. The emotion and physical addiction to alcohol was almost more than Carol could bear. She wanted to go into Happy's so bad that it was just killing her. Her body and her emotions were screaming for her to go inside shouting just one drink . . . . just one drink . . . . you deserve this . . . . don't you want to go and be happy . . . . but Carol stood her ground. Whenever she tried to quit in the past Carol was unable to do it on her own. This time she had a team to help her—Jesus, the Holy Spirit and Ann Lorenzo. She cried out to Jesus for help and was able to drive out of the parking lot and never look back. Jesus and the Holy Spirit slowly took that addiction out of Carol's heart—but it was still a real fight.

One by one most of Carol's old drinking buddies fell to the wayside—or she outgrew them. She would see some of the girls from time to time but her life was changing and the alcoholic bond that once held them together no longer existed. Carol was now bonded to a higher power that was not present in the lives of her old drinking buddies. The two or three friends that Carol still sees from her past also have changed their lives for the better.

When both Carol and George went to their respective AA meetings they were introduced to the following twelve steps of Alcoholics Anonymous:

1. We admitted we were powerless over alcohol—that our lives had been unmanageable.

2. Came to believe that a Power greater that ourselves could restore us to sanity.

3. Made a decision to turn our will and our lives to the care of God *as we understood him.*

4. Made a searching and fearless moral inventory of ourselves.

5. Admitted to God, to ourselves, and another human being the exact nature of our wrongs.

6. Were entirely ready to have God remove all these defects of character.

7. Humbly asked Him to remove our shortcomings.

8. Made a list of all persons we have harmed, and became willing to make amends to them all.

9. Made direct amends to such people whenever possible, except when to do so would injure them or others.

10. Continued to take personal inventory and when we were wrong promptly admitted it.

11. Sought thru prayer and meditation to improve our conscious contact with God, *as we understood Him*, praying for the knowledge of His will for us and the power to carry that out.

12. Having had a spiritual awakening as the result of these steps, we tried to carry this message to alcoholics, and to practice these principles in all our affairs.

As Carol went to these meetings she continued to learn about these 12 steps. It was about a year before she worked on all twelve. After about a year of sobriety Carol experienced a sense of clearness she had not noticed before.

After Carol's first year she began to sponsor other girls. She was active in AA for the next fifteen years and helped to bring many persons to sobriety. Carol also started leading meetings and spoke in front of many groups over the years. God has opened many doors for Carol and has given her the opportunity to tell her story with Jesus at the center and to share the gospel of Jesus Christ. But as we shall see—God is not done with Carol just yet.

CHAPTER SIXTEEN

Love Is In The Air

Be of good courage, and he shall strengthen your heart, All you who hope in the Lord.

Psalm 31:24

Now faith is the substance of things hoped for, the evidence of things not seen

Hebrews 11:1

George and Carol first became acquainted with each other around 1978 or 1979 when they both were attending an AA meeting. When they each heard the other say "Hi, my name is _____ and I am an alcoholic" they had no idea that God had special plans for them and that since before the beginning of time God had set the plans in motion for them to one day be joined as one. Let's now hear what each of them has to say about the events which led to the fulfillment of God's continued plans for their lives.

George

Like most men, George is a man of few words. His actions speak louder than his words. He is by nature a quiet and reflective man. I gave George and Carol a page full of questions asking about their relationship, how they met, whether or not it was love at first sight, etc. George provided me with about a half a page of short to the point answers while Carol provided me with three pages of a highly detailed account of their lives from that first AA meeting to their wedding vows and beyond. Each of them, however, bring a unique perspective of how God has worked in their lives and continues to do so as these very words are written.

According to George, he was engaged to another woman when he first saw Carol in the late 1970's at their AA meetings. That relationship soured and soon after that George began dating Carol. George was still living at 18715 Pawnee Avenue when he met Carol and he was still working at United Musical Instruments (formerly known as King Musical Instruments).

As George continued to date Carol he found that they had a great deal in common. Although George had not yet been saved, he and Carol shared a common bond of sobriety. Both he and Carol were clean and sober and went to a number of meetings together.

George found Carol very easy to talk to on a variety of subjects. As soon as they started dating George shared his feelings about his murdered daughter Amy with Carol. Carol, who did have a saving relationship with Christ when she met George, took a keen interest in George's telling her about Amy because she knew Amy was a Christian and that Amy held a special place in George's heart. This was one of the things that attracted Carol to George.

George and Carol also had many conversations about salvation and what George needed to do to be "born again." Although George had known about Christ ever since he was a Catholic he never stepped forward and admitted he was a sinner and invited Christ into his heart. In his youth George had been an altar boy and received all his sacraments (i.e. baptism, Holy Communion, confirmation and holy matrimony) and did indeed honor God as his Holy Father. But something was missing—that special bond one enjoys with Christ when we invite Him into our hearts and the second helper (the Holy Spirit) indwells us. When George finally did invite Christ into his heart on May 15, 1983 he realized that he did not really know Christ in the past.

George and Carol were married on October 1, 1983. George's brother Jerome was his best man. George attributes their marital longevity to the fact that both he and Carol place God in the center of their lives. George believes with all his heart that God guides Carol and him on a daily basis and they both try to follow His direction in their lives. George acknowledges that God and His loving Son are the head of their relationship.

Carol

Carol had first met George at their AA meetings in the late 1970's. At that time George was just another member who, like Carol, was in a wrestling match with the demons who had caused alcohol to be their drug of choice in the first place. When they had both met in AA each of them had been involved with somebody else. About a year after they had met George became engaged to another woman and Carol was dating as well.

Prior to entering AA, Carol had dated a man on and off for ten years with the hope of one day being his wife—but this was not meant to be. In 1977 Carol met a man in AA who was the same age as she was (33) and they dated for the next couple of years. They had a great time together and went to a number of AA meetings together. Carol came to know Christ as her Lord and Savior on July 12, 1976 and was released from the bondage of alcohol on August 24, 1976. Carol and her new "friend" had a great deal in common. Both of them were "saved" and both of them were in AA. He was a Christian man and highly educated and held a PhD and came from a wealthy family. They went to Bible study together and AA and picnics and spent a great deal of time together. Their relationship could be defined as more than friends but not exactly boyfriend and girlfriend. In 1980 he was transferred to Michigan and their relationship just kind of dissolved due to the distance between them. Carol had wished that the relationship had grown prior to his transfer but it was just not meant to be. While this initially appeared to perhaps have been a match made in heaven God had other plans for Carol.

By 1981 George and his girlfriend had broken off their relationship and had stopped dating. In May of 1981, while Carol was still working at St. Luke's Hospital, George had asked her on a date. They went to the Front Row Theater (which was the place to be in Cleveland in the 1980's) and saw Engelbert Humperdinck live.

Carol recalls that several times George wanted to send her flowers while they were dating and the practical side of her told George not to because cut flowers didn't last long and they were so expensive. Carol now asks herself what was she thinking.

Carol and George dated for two years and got engaged on May 11, 1983. According to Carol, the day after they got engaged the Lord really dealt with Carol because George was not saved yet. The Holy Spirit would not leave Carol alone. She was not at peace and was being convicted all day long. Carol called her cousin who had led her to Christ in 1976 and asked him what she should do. He told Carol what she already knew—that she should not marry George because he was not a Christian and scripture told her that two people who are unevenly yoked should not be joined together. As a Christian, Carol wanted God's blessing on their relationship and their subsequent marriage and she knew that she would not have this blessing if what she was proposing to do was contrary to God's word. Carol could not get any sleep that night as she was sick over this because she knew what she had to do.

The next morning she had made up her mind that she had to honor God's word and that if she was going to build a relationship with anybody that this was something that she was going to do right—and do it God's way. Armed with her spiritual conviction Carol went over to George's house and between tears told him that she could not marry him because they were not one in Christ. George did not really know what Carol was talking about but he knew that she was serious. They talked for quite a while and George asked Carol what she wanted him to do. For some reason it did not occur to Carol to witness to George at that moment and ask him to ask Christ into his heart. Perhaps the emotion of the moment clouded Carol's thinking. Carol and George had talked about God all the time prior to this moment in time and though she had hoped that he had somehow backed into salvation she knew in her heart of hearts that this was not true and his question of "what must I do?" confirmed her deepest fear. That the man she loved and was engaged to marry was somebody she could not marry under any circumstance—it would just be wrong and she was not about to put her needs ahead of the commandments of her Lord.

Later that day Carol called a Pastor who was a former Catholic and had recently started a church service in a school gym in Eastlake, Ohio. Having been a former Catholic Carol knew that this Pastor would understand their situation. The Pastor invited George to come and visit his services on Wednesday May 18, 1983. George did attend service that night and invited Christ into his heart (see the next chapter for full details).

Carol and George were married on October 1, 1983 and Carol's sister, Joan, was her maid of honor. Seventy-five of their friends and family witnessed the blessed event.

George and Carol were married in the new Villa Angela Academy chapel. When the new building was built a huge old stump from the former building was brought over to the new building and made into an altar in Amy's honor because Amy was partially responsible for the new academy being built. George and Carol were married in plain sight of this honorary altar.

By the time Carol and George had gotten married all of the children were out of the house. Within a year or so of Carol and George's wedding his daughter Annette and his son James were also married.

Amy had been a part of Carol's life everyday since she first made acquaintances with George. George and Carol continued to talk about Amy during their dating. When Carol found out Amy was a Christian she was excited to hear all about her. Even today Carol still enjoys learning more and more about Amy and the lives she touched during her time on this earth. Carol can't wait to meet Amy in heaven and neither can I. Carol feels like she knows Amy so well and I am getting to know her better as well. Carol and George started going to the "Amy Sambula Assembly" when they were dating and still do go every January.

Like Carol, and countless others of you who are reading this book, we had been involved in a number of relationships before being introduced to the person that God hand picked for us. Looking back at the wake of bodies left behind during our dating experiences, I am sure that all of us are glad that God certainly has more sense of who we need to fulfill the role of helpmate in our lives than we did during our pre-marital dating days.

Just think what it took to get Carol and George together. On George's side of the ledger we have the death of his daughter, the death of his wife, near death experiences with alcohol, his sobriety, an engagement that ended, and his salvation. On Carol's side of the ledger we have a ten year relationship that did not end in marriage, a "match made in heaven" that did not work out, her battle with alcohol and subsequent sobriety, and her salvation. Despite an age difference of twelve years, and countless other factors that could have plagued their thirty year relationship, their relationship has endured because of two reasons. First of all their relationship was planned for and ordained by God and secondly both Carol and George have come to realize that they are each a gift to each other hand selected by God for their mutual pleasure here on earth. May each of you who are reading this book be blessed with this appreciation of your hand selected mate.

Today both Carol and George honorably say that without a doubt Jesus is the center and head of their marriage. According to Carol marriage takes three! The following is a poem that was given to Carol and George on their wedding day almost twenty-eight years ago:

MARRIAGE TAKES THREE

I once thought marriage took
Just two to make a go
But now I am convinced
It takes the Lord also.

And not one marriage fails
Where Christ is asked to enter
As lovers come together
With Jesus at the center.

But marriage seldom thrives
And homes are incomplete
Till He is welcomed there
To help avert defeat.

In homes where God is first
It's obvious to see
Those unions really work
For marriage still takes three.

And so it has been for George and Carol.

CHAPTER SEVENTEEN

The Angels Rejoice

The Lord is my strength and song and He has become my salvation. He is my God and I will praise him.

Exodus 15:2

For by grace you have been saved through faith, and that not of yourselves, it is the gift of God

Ephesians 2:8

"And when he comes home, he calls together his friends and neighbors, saying to them, Rejoice with me for I have found my sheep which was lost!"

"I say to you likewise there will be more joy in heaven over one sinner who repents than over ninety-nine persons who need no repentance."

Luke 15:6-7

Of all the dates in life there are several that tend to stay with you for a lifetime. Your birthday and your anniversary are two that come to mind. For those of us who are believers in Christ there is a third date that is burned in our memory banks until we get to glory—the date we fell to our knees and admitted we were sinners and invited Christ into our hearts. For George that date was May 18, 1983.

George recalls that on that particular date he and his fiancé, Carol Zimmerman, went to Jefferson Elementary School in Eastlake, Ohio to attend church services held by a Pastor that Carol had known. This Pastor held his services in the gymnasium of the school and in the middle of the wooden basketball court a large "J" was painted on the floor which was the "J" for Jefferson Elementary. Being a former Catholic, the Pastor spoke to George about the concept of being "born again" and asked George if he was ready to admit he was a sinner and to invite Christ into his heart. George and the Pastor talked for a little while longer and then a kneeler was brought out and placed directly over that "J" in the middle of the gymnasium floor. George got down on his knees and admitted he was a sinner and invited Jesus Christ into his heart and asked Jesus to be his Lord and Savior. George recalls that as he did this he broke out in a cold sweat and that the moment the "J" in the middle of the floor stood for Jesus and not Jefferson.

George was now one with Christ and he now had the Holy Spirit in his heart as a second helper. The pain and anguish that alcohol addiction and death brought into George's life did not immediately vanish. His tears were not dried immediately. The sense of loss of life was still with George and some of this pain he still carries with him to this day. What George now discovered was that the journey that God had taken him on up to this point was necessary for his salvation. That God had always been in control, was in control at this moment, and would control George's path from the point of his salvation until God calls him to His side. George now knows the end of the story. He knows the final chapter of his life. No matter what this world had in store George he could endure because he knew that one day he would be returning to his home in heaven.

CHAPTER EIGHTEEN

Twenty Years Later

Authors Note: In writing this book George and Carol shared many treasures that George had gathered over the years as a testimony to the love that Amelia infected others with during her journey here on earth. I felt both privileged and honored to share these memories with George and Carol. I came across a typed document that the Principal of Amy's High School wrote as a speech to commemorate the 20th anniversary of Amy's going home to be with the Lord. The type written text of the speech reads as follows:

Girls, I must truthfully tell you that I prayed to Amy and asked her to bless me with a way to convey to you something about her that each of you could easily imitate and follow. I hope that my talk will do just that.

Introduction:

Today, November 22, 1989 is the 20th anniversary of the death of Amelia Theresa Sambula, fondly know as Amy (Sambula). I will endeavor to *"Remember Amy"* and try to share with you the Blessing of the Memory that was our Amy! I chose to do this through the letters of her Name and what I believe they stand for,

A—Let us look at the first letter of her name . . . . *A.* The word Amy is derived from the Latin word *"Amore—to love* and from this we get the words: amiable, attractive, agreeable—words that fit Amy perfectly, for she was lovingly agreeable and amiable (true friend) to each of the girls who prided themselves in being a Villa Angela girl! As we progress through the other letters of her name you will see these characteristics come to life.

***M**—The letter "M" stands for MATURE* and Amy was a mature *Christian woman* who gave all of her time, spirit and love to foster an atmosphere of Christian giving at V.A. (Villa Angela), hence what better time to award the Amy Sambula scholarship than Thanksgiving time.

The letter "M" also stands for MEMORY—the memory that was Amy "whose heart was filled with pride in our V.A. . . . ." These words were uttered by Amy in one of her addresses to the student-body when she was elected council president—on October 13, 1969—just five weeks before her untimely death.

***Y**—The letter "Y" reminds me of her YOUTH* and presents me with the picture of her tossing her YELLOW blonde curls as she inspired the girls to work together to clean up the campus to make V.A. beautiful and then have us bring bags of leaves, twigs, etc. to the gym and join in celebrating "PROJECT CLEANUP." She sat down on the edge of the stage, feet hanging down and led us in a great song-fest, tossing her yellow curls to the rhythm of the music. Her enthusiasm was youthfully electrifying and the girls followed her lead. If the Principal hadn't intervened I think that we would still be singing!!!

***S**—The letter "S"* is the first letter of Amy's last name and it reminds me of Amy as our STUDENT COUNCIL PRESIDENT. *As such* she worked to make our V.A. a real, ideal Christian Community. During one of her last addresses to the girls she told them that in attaining this ideal there must be a certain amount of "self-sacrifice." Could we say that her death *was that* sacrifice or offering for us?
. . . . "for to everything there is a season and a time to every purpose under the heavens . . . . a time to be born and a time to die."

The letter "S" also stands for *SERVICE and SHARING of talents.* Amy exhibited these gifts in her retreat work with the V.A. girls and with the C.Y.O. groups of her parish.

Another "S" denotes the sensitive and generous *SPIRIT* which was Amy. I remember her saying to us over the P.A. "This morning I was thinking about the *Purple Palace,* the *Float in the Parade,* our *Leadership Workshop and Retreat* and my whole heart was filled with Pride in our V.A."

Amy kept trying even when *"her arms were too weary to reach the unreachable star"*—she *never* was too busy to help someone.

The purple palace that Amy referred to was the old Villa Angela. We called it the Castle but Amy called it the "Purple Palace." *The Float*: Under Amy's urging, leadership and guidance V.A. entered a float in the Columbus Day Parade downtown that October of 1969. The wording under the float stated: "Another New World Discovered" and under the picture of the float in the Yearbook the girls added—"another New World discovered through Amy."

A—stands for ASK. Amy *asked* much of us *and she gave much*—and out of this ASKING and giving she wove great leadership.

M—is for MUSIC: Amy made Music with her trumpet. She was our V.A. Musician and the first V.A. girl to play in the St. Joe's band. She played lead trumpet in both their concert and stage bands.

"M" is also for her MIND: She used her mind through hard study to attain first and second honors in her Freshman, Sophomore and Junior Years and in the first Quarter of her Senior Year. She applied to Ohio Dominican College and St. Mary's College in Notre Dame, Indiana in October and following her death V.A. learned of her acceptance at both colleges.

B—stands for BRIGHTNESS, the brightness that was Amy in our lives. She challenged the members of the *Student Council and the study body as well* to creativity—by being creative herself.

"B" also stands for *BELIEVER*. Amy believed in God as her trusted friend on whom she could always rely. She was a very prayerful girl who drew her strength from God. To those who denied belief in a personal God, Amy witnessed with her words and life that the Christ she knew was a PERSON FOR OTHERS.

U—stands for UNITE—to join together. Amy was a great *UNIFIER*. She worked daily to help us all *"be of one mind and one heart!"* through the various V.A. school projects that she initiated such as:

1. SCHOOL FLOAT IN PROJECT CLEANUP
2. CLASS SKITS
3. TEACHER APPRECIATION DAYS
4. THE SCHOOL ORCHESTRA/BAND
5. THE SCHOOL FLOAT IN THE COLUMBUS DAY PARADE
etc.

L—stands for LEADER. Amy was a natural leader—and her leadership experience to quote AMY "has helped me grow tremendously as a person. I have been able to meet and share many things with many people—one of which is *learning* how much we need each other."

A—This last letter of Amy's name stands for ASIAN STUDIES, a class that Amy thoroughly enjoyed and the medium through which I came to know Amy so well.

"A" also stands for ADAPTABILITY—that quality that spelled Amy's willingness *to adjust to suggestions of the faculty and students* and to mesh the two together to form a unified community. *"PRAISE GOD, we'll work it out,"* became her famous by-line!

In CONCLUSION—On November 8th of this year I called and spoke with Jackie Trost who was the Vice President of the Student Council under Amy and who succeeded her in that capacity when Amy died. Without eulogizing Amy, Jackie said that she remembers Amy as a person who enjoyed fun, who had her share of teen-age problems like the rest of us, *but she had a charisma that drew people to her, and that charisma was the inner peace that she possessed.* Amy's enthusiasm and zest for life rubbed off on you when you were with her. *She knew who she was.* She had a genuine love of God beyond her years and she expressed this love and her faith openly in her witnessing at prayer meetings and during retreats. *Amy showed the Way to Peace to the V.A. student body* and with her trumpet she was like the Pied-Piper leading girls to GOD.

Author's Note: Again I'd like to thank George and Carol Sambula for sharing this treasured document for me which I captured word-for-word just as it was written over twenty years ago. I'd also like to close this Chapter with the words from the song "God of All":

God of all mercy, God of all grace,
    God of all wonder and fame.
Wonderful, Counselor, Savior and Friend,
    Your Kingdom, it has no end.
And forever You reign, and forever You reign.
    Oceans cry out and the stars declare
Who you are, who you are.

All of the splendors of heaven unveil
    Who you are, who you are
Lord you are, Lord you are . . . .

CHAPTER NINETEEN

Villa Angela Honor Roll

For You formed my inward parts;
You covered me in my mother's womb.

I praise You, for I am fearfully and wonderfully made;
Marvelous are your works,
And *that* my soul knows very well.

My frame was not hidden from you,
When I was made in secret,
And skillfully wrought in the lowest parts of the earth.

Your eyes saw my substance, and being yet unformed.
And in Your book they all were written,
The days fashioned for me,
When *as yet there were* none of them.

Psalm 139:13-16

In the year 2003 the Amy Sambula Scholarship was re-instituted to continue to provide support for a young woman student at Villa Angela who best mirrors the spirit, enthusiasm, dedication and commitment that was so much a part of the life of Amy while she was a student at Villa Angela. As part of the re-birth of this program former classmates were asked to reflect on their memories of Amy. Their thoughts are noted below:

Amy was a senior when I was a junior. I remember her as a strong leader, great musician, but "everybody's friend." Though I did not know her well, she made me feel that way. Then at the end of my junior year, the first Amy Sambula Scholarship was awarded. I knew that it would be an honor to receive it, yet I was aware of the financial needs of our large family. Those needs prompted me to pray to receive it. Imagine my joy at hearing my name called at the assembly that day! The Lord blessed our needs, plus allowed me to have the qualities as the first recipient of the Amy Sambula Scholarship. *(**Mary Anne Krahe Palm**—Class of 1971).*

The small group that made up the Villa Angela band had practiced for weeks to prepare for the concert, so to this day I am not sure what happened the night of the performance. Somewhere during one of the songs we got "out of sync" and suddenly found ourselves producing a cacophony of notes. One by one, we realized what had happened and stopped playing, looking to the director and trying to quickly find where we were supposed to be. Out of this din came a loud clear melody leading us back to harmony. It was Amy on her trumpet, asking us to recover and continue with the show that we so desperately wanted to give the audience. With Amy's leadership we did recover, finishing not only that piece, but also giving our best for the rest of the concert. This was so like Amy, to see a need and then reach out and lead the way.

Like the shooting of President John F. Kennedy, or the events of September 11th, the death of Amy Sambula was a watershed moment for every girl at Villa Angela that year. No doubt each of us remembers where we were and what we were doing when we heard about Amy's murder. Maybe in some way we all carry some of the pain and disbelief with us to this day. But we also remember the joy and hope that was Amy. You didn't need to be part of her crowd to know you liked her and respected her. She was one of those special people you meet in life that just brings sunshine to everything they do and to everyone they meet. And maybe that's the legacy that Amy gave us—a reminder to see good in others, to see the joy of life and to make our faith real every day. *(**Margaret (Peg) Mosphens Geffert**—Class of 1971).*

When I think of Amy when we were seniors—I always remember her constant smile and the way she got along with "everybody" in all the different cliques! Everyone loved her! I worked at Red Robin's clothing store with her and we would share funny stories! I mostly remember one day when we all were walking down the "long, long" V.A. driveway—we were talking about how we loved "Marvin Gaye and Tammy Terrell!" Amy was an inspiration to everyone who knew her! *(Patricia E. Fuerst—Class of 1970).*

I remember walking home from school with Amy. She was always so happy. I remember wearing white gloves and being in her honor guard at her beautiful funeral. *(Megan McGrath Cohen—Class of 1971).*

I remember her positive attitude and kind spirit! *(Kathleen Hocevar—Class of 1971).*

She sat next to me in French class. Always had a smile on her face. Had a kind word for everyone. *(Georgianni Basilone Moss—Class of 1971).*

She was a beautiful person inside and out. I truly miss her. *(Mary Margaret McHugh Dacar—Class of 1971).*

I remember that Amy was kind to everyone. She never had an unkind word to say about any human being. She was friendly, beautiful, smart, talented and a true leader. *(Lynn Yohem Perry—Class of 1972).*

I was recently in town and driving down E. 185th Street—when I started thinking about Amy but could not remember her last name. I then received your (VASJ's) request in the mail. After 33 years, I still remember that tragedy and its unusualness at that time. May Amy never be forgotten. *(Joanne Kinn—Class of 1971).*

Who can forget Amy? She was bright and sweet and good at almost everything she tried—the books, the French, the big musical instrument she lugged around after school. But it just wasn't her goodness I remember. Almost a relief that she was not terribly athletic, but you guessed it—she was . . . a very good sport—came to play volleyball, basketball with the rest of the girls in after school pickup or intramural games—she was there along with the rest of her class. Of course you couldn't help but love this girl. *(Mary Palmer Hollowell—Class of 1969).*

Note that each year Villa Anegla-St. Joseph High School awards the Amy Sambula scholarship to the student who best exemplifies the qualities that George's daughter possessed i.e. generosity, Christian concern, and sacrifice for others. Until the merge of Villa Angela with St. Joseph's High School (a former all boys Catholic School) the scholarship assembly was originally called "The Amy Sambula Assembly." With the merger of these two schools this event has been called the "Founder's Day Celebration." Since the Amy Sambula scholarship program began in 1970, many more former students who have lost their lives have been remembered in this annual event.

George and Carol Sambula went to this event on January 27, 2011 and George had the honor of presenting a scholarship in the amount of $5,000.00 to the worthy recipient. This year Amy's class of 1970 contributed $5,000.00 with other donations coming from other former classmates, friends, and family. Like the gift of salvation we receive from Christ, the gift from Amy's memory will also be used to change lives for years to come.

Author's note: On March 4, 2011 I was listening to an oldies station on the car radio as I was driving from Washington, D.C, back home to Cleveland and a Marvin Gaye/Tammy Terrell song came on entitled "How Sweet it is to be Loved by You." I started thinking about Amy and her girlfriend noted above (Patricia E. Fuerst) listening to this duo and then thought of Amy. I thought it would have been nice to have met her here on earth and am looking forward to spending time with her in glory.

CHAPTER TWENTY

The Power of Prayer

Blessed be God, Who has not turned away my prayer, Nor His mercy from me!

Psalm 66:20

The Lord is far from the wicked; But He hears the prayers of the righteous

Proverbs 15:29

Then another angel, having a golden censer, came and stood at the altar. He was given much incense, that he should offer it with the prayers of all the saints upon the golden altar which was before the throne.

Revelation 8:3

Author's Note: One of the privileges of writing this book was sharing Amelia's life with George and Carol and obtaining an appreciation of the person Amelia was and what Christ meant to her in her life. This is best illustrated by the following note that Amelia wrote in a spiral notebook on the subject of prayer.

> So too, God always hears our prayers,
> but not as or when we like. He wants
> us to have deep faith.

We sometimes stop trusting but keep
praying with no faith in our prayers
(story of Zechariah).
God hears our very first prayer which
may be the result of divine inspiration.

Have you ever wondered why it hurts so
much to pray? . . . . because prayer
is being born into a new life and being
born is painful.

Words at times kill prayer:
They will us, too, whereas realities feed us.
So do words if they're real—but often
they're empty—they weary us without
being fruit.

Our words hide things instead of
revealing them . . . . Words can screen
reality from view.

It was a weary prayer that saved
the world. Jesus prayed a prayer of desolation.
He suffered enough from weariness enough to
die, more than we'll ever suffer from it or
from the desire to escape and do our
own will.

Our wearied prayer will save the world
and us.

On July 23, 2011 I read a book by Pastor Todd Burpo entitled "Heaven is for Real." Todd Burpo is the Pastor of Crossroads Wesleyan Church in Imperial, Nebraska. On March 3, 2003 Pastor Burpo's not quite four year old son, Colton, was gravely ill in a children's hospital suffering from a ruptured appendix and a serious abscess as a result of this rupture. Prior to this hospitalization Pastor Burpo suffered a severely broken leg, kidney stones, and a cancer scare.

Pastor Burpo found a quiet place in the hospital while Colton was being operated on and tears of rage fell upon his cheeks as he had a heart to heart chat with God. He asked God that after the leg, the kidney stone, and the mastectomy; is this how God was going to let him celebrate the end of his time of testing. Pastor Burpo yelled at God and told Him that He was not going to take his son.

Some time after Colton had successfully come through his surgery, Pastor Burpo and his wife had been told by Colton that he had been to heaven during his surgery and that he had seen Jesus. The book takes the reader through a fascinating journey of Colton revealing a number of his experiences while in heaven during his operation.

In one scene in the book Calton revealed that he yelled for his father to come to his side after the operation because Jesus had told him to do so in an answer to his father's prayers. Pastor Burpo's knees felt weak when he remembered praying alone, raging at God, and praying desperately for God to spare his son's life. He remembered how scared he was agonizing over whether his son would make it through surgery. He wondered whether Colton would live long enough so that he could see his precious face again. Pastor Burpo said those were the longest, darkest ninety minutes of his life.

Now Colton revealed to his father that Jesus did hear his prayers and answered them personally. After he had yelled at God, chastised him, and questioned his wisdom and his faithfulness God bestowed mercy upon Todd Burpo and his son, Colton.

We do serve an awesome God who does answer our prayers.

To learn more about Colton Burpo's special journey to heaven I urge to you read Pastor Burpo's book and visit Colton and the Burpo family at www.heavenisforreal.net.

CHAPTER TWENTY ONE

Forgiveness

Let all bitterness, wrath, anger, clamor, and evil speaking be put away from you, with all malice.

And be kind to one another, tenderhearted, forgiving one another, just as God in Christ also forgave you.

Ephesians 4:31-32

Then Peter came to Him and said, "Lord, how often shall my brother sin against me, and I forgive him? Up to seven times?" Jesus said to him, "I do not say to you, up to seven times, but up to seventy times seven."

Matthew 18:21-22

I happened to be flipping through the Reader's Digest a few months ago in the dentist's office and came upon an interesting article on forgiveness. In this particular case, like that of George and Joan Sambula, Betty Ferguson's daughter, Debbie, was senselessly murdered in 1975 at age 16 by her high school English teacher, Ray Payne. Just like George had done Betty Ferguson drank herself to sleep every night. Day after day Betty cursed her young daughter's killer and nearly drove herself mad asking why again and again and found no answer. She was consumed by hate and suffered constantly with everything from daily headaches to constant back pain.

In 1981 Betty Ferguson attended the funeral of her sister and the following line from the Lord's Prayer stuck with her: "forgive those who trespass against us." Betty visited her daughter's tombstone which read "What the world needs now is love, sweet love."

Shortly thereafter Betty Ferguson was repeating the words "I am willing to forgive Ray" over and over again and it became her mantra. Within months Betty wrote to Ray Payne in prison saying that she was done being mad with him and asked if she could come and share her journey with him.

In 1986—eleven years after her daughter was taken from her—Betty Ferguson visited Ray Payne in prison. She told him what her daughter had meant to her and how lost and heartbroken she had been. Betty said that Ray listened and they both cried and she left that prison a different person. She said that her heart felt soft and light and warm.

Betty Ferguson now says that forgiveness is the greatest gift she ever gave to herself and her children and that her having forgiven Ray Payne has been part of an incredible healing journey that has saved her life.

The more I am involved in the authorship of this project the more I feel the hand of God and His Holy Spirit guiding my every step and my every word. The following portion of the book on continued forgiveness helps to illustrate this point.

When my son was in his early teens he worked with a young landscaper named Dave Fakadej who gave a number of young boys in our rural area their first glimpse at what it was like to have a real job. Dave instilled a keen work ethic in a number of these boys as they transformed from boys into men. Never in my wildest dreams did I ever think that landscaper Dave would someday become Dr. David Fakadej and play a role in my book. While I never dreamed this—God knew all along that Dr. Dave would in fact play such a role.

An article in our local paper, the Spirit of Bainbridge, entitled "Forgiveness Improves Immune Function" was written by none other than Dr. David Fakadej. Dr. Dave stated in his article that true forgiveness brings peace of mind, reduces chronic stress and anxiety, reduces stress hormones, and boosts immune, reproductive and digestive functions. According to Dr. Dave true forgiveness does not ask the impossible (i.e. forgive the terrible deed that may have been perpetrated against you or a loved one) it asks that you have willingness to let go of that which causes you pain and suffering. Dr. Dave says that the choice is ours.

The genesis of this book began with a Sunday school conversation with George and Carol Sambula in the Spring of 2010. At the end of my Sunday school lesson I had a conversation with George over whether or not he had forgiven the man who took Amy's life so many years ago. George told me that he had forgiven him. I must admit I was initially taken back by this answer and asked him how was he able to do so. George told me straight away that he had become the man and the Christian that God wanted him to be today by being formed and shaped by the trials that God put him through. George pointed to the fact that his victory over alcohol addiction and his coming to invite Jesus into his heart as his Savior was directly linked to Amy's death and Joan's death and the assorted number of other trials that he had endured by the grace of God and His loving Son.

While Betty Ferguson found comfort in one portion of the Lord's Prayer: "forgive those who trespass against us" George also found comfort in another portion of this prayer which says "Thy will be done on earth as it is in Heaven."

CHAPTER TWENTY TWO

03.20.11

You have been so good to me,
You have been so good to me.
I came here broken, you make me whole.
You have been so good, You have been so good.
You have been so good to me.

You have been so good to me,
You have been so good to me.
I came here mourning, You gave me joy.
You have been so good, You have been so good.
You have been so good to me.

From the song "You Have Been So Good"

But Jesus looked at them and said, "With man this is impossible, but with God all things are possible."

Matthew 19:26

In March of 2011 George and Carol announced to the congregation that George's son, Georgie, had been diagnosed with cancer. This had sent chills up and down George's spine. He has lost his first wife, Joan, to that dreaded disease so many years ago and now that disease was knocking on his door again. The diagnosis didn't look good. The x-rays showed green in the lymph nodes of Georgie and when cancer is normally located in this area of the body it spreads like wildfire. The church bulletin on March 6,

2011 under ***IN OUR PRAYERS THIS WEEK*** read as follows: George Sambula's Son, George—healing from lung cancer.

The doctors were to operate on Georgie on March 15, 2011 to look and see what they could see. Carol had asked in Sunday's service on March 13, 2011 that we pray for George and his son and that when the doctors opened up Georgie that there be no cancer at all. When we opened the church bulletin on March 20, 2011 under prayer needs the bulletin read: George Sambula's son, George—Praise The Lord! Not lung cancer, healing.

The doctors discovered that Georgie did not have lung cancer but was suffering from a very serious, but curable, infection and will be as good as new. Did Georgie ever have lung cancer and cancer in his lymph nodes? We really don't know for sure. All we do know is that George and Carol trusted God to do His will on this earth and He did.

CHAPTER TWENTY THREE

It Is Well With My Soul

As for God, His way is perfect;
The word of the Lord is proven;
He is a shield to all who trust in Him.

2 Samuel 22:31

Oh, give thanks to the Lord, for he is good!
Because his mercy endures forever
Let Israel now say, "His mercy endures forever."
Let the house of Aaron now say, "His mercy endures forever."
Let those who fear the Lord now say,
"His mercy endures forever."

Psalm 118:1-4

And He was withdrawn from them about
a stone's throw, and He knelt down and prayed,

Saying, "Father, if it is Your will take this cup
from Me; nevertheless not My will, but Yours, be done."

Luke 22:41-42 NKJ

On March 26, 2011 our Church celebrated the life of Jackie Hrvatin who was the mother of one of our members, Nadine Hrvatin. At the close of the memorial service our Pastor's wife, Bethany, gave an inspirational rendition of an old time hymn, "It is well with my soul." The stirring words contain the following refrain:

> When peace like a river, attendeth my way;
> When sorrows like sea billows roll;
> Whatever my lot, Thou has taught me to know,
> It is well, it is well with my soul.
>
> Though Satan should buffet, though trial should come,
> Let this blessed assurance control,
> That Christ hath regarded my helpless estate,
> And hath shed his own blood for my soul.

The author of this song, Horatio Spafford, suffered a great many tragedies before putting these comforting words to paper and ink.

On October 8, 1871 the great Chicago fire swept through the city leaving in its path great destruction. Horatio Spafford, a prominent Chicago lawyer, who had invested heavily in real estate, had almost everything he owned destroyed by this fire.

In 1873 Spafford planned a family vacation to England and sent his wife Anna and their four children Anna (age 11), Margaret Lee (age nine), Elizabeth (age five) and Tanetta (age two) on ahead aboard the steamship *Ville de Havre*. On November 22, 1873 while crossing the Atlantic their ship was struck by an iron sailing vessel and two hundred and twenty-six persons lost their lives, including the four Spafford daughters. Upon arriving in England Anna Spafford sent a telegram to her husband Horatio beginning with the words "saved alone."

Spafford then sailed to England and while going over the watery graves of his four daughters penned the words noted above.

Often our lives are not as we planned or hoped or dreamed. Certainly George Sambula had no inkling that he would be called upon to surrender the life of his daughter, Amy, to God at such a young age. But as George looks back in retrospect he says that he had to go through all that God had allowed him to endure so that he could become the man that God wanted him to become. As your sea billows roll around you, may you find comfort in these trials faced by and triumphed over by Horatio Spafford, George Sambula and countless others who have placed their faith in God and their trust in Jesus Christ.

CHAPTER TWENTY FOUR

In a Mind's Eye

Trust in the Lord with all your heart, and lean not on your own understanding

Proverbs 3:5

For God has not given us a spirit of fear, but of power and of love and of a sound mind

2 Timothy 1:7

The mind is one unique organ that God has created for us. It stores multitudes of information and at a moment's notice these nuggets of information come racing back to us. Perhaps a certain smell or a time of the year or a certain color triggers memories—both good and bad.

George and I were talking after Sunday school in early July of 2011 and he told me that a recent article in the news about the Anthony Sowell trial brought back memories of the jury coming to see the site of Amy's murder. An article appeared in the Cleveland Plain Dealer on June 28, 2011 describing how the jury in the Sowell murder case viewed the scene of the site of eleven murders committed by Anthony Sowell. At the time of the article Anthony Sowell was accused of murdering eleven women on Cleveland's eastside and the jury came to the scene as part of the trial.

George told me that in the case of his murdered daughter after the jury was selected the prosecutor had the jury bussed to the area where Amy's body had lain. An outline of her body where she had laid after she was shot had been placed on the ground by the authorities for the jury to see. According to George the jury examined the murder scene and left. George said that he and his wife were home at the time and witnessed the whole thing as it happened. The murder scene was no more than ten feet from the Sambula home.

CHAPTER TWENTY FIVE

300 Paces, 28 seconds, 10 Feet

For He knows our frame; He remembers that we are dust. As for man, his days are like grass; as a flower of the field, so he flourishes. For the wind passes over it and it is gone, and its place remembers it no more,

Psalm 103:14-16

And let the peace of God rule in your hearts, to which also you were called in one body; and be thankful.

Colossians 3:15

After hearing George's story about the jury visiting his family home I felt the need to take my co-worker (and my proofreader) on a road trip to the Sambula neighborhood during our lunch break. As we drove to the Sambula's old neighborhood off of E. 185th Street near the shoreway, my co-worker asked me where we were going and I said it was a secret. Driving on Route 90 east out of downtown I could not help but think that this was the very same route that homicide Detectives John Kaminsky and Harold Murphy took over forty years ago when they investigated Amy's murder. I wondered if they had the same apprehension as I did as my co-worker and I made our way out of downtown Cleveland on a 15 minute 10.44 mile trek to Sambula's old neighborhood.

As I exited Route 90 East onto E. 185th Street my co-worker asked if we were going to the murder scene and I said yes we were. She then got a little quiet.

We drove down E. 185th Street searching for the address of the former Red Robin clothing store where Amy had worked so many years ago. I knew that the Red Robin chain had long since left the Cleveland area and I wondered what we would find in its place. We pulled up to the curb and got out of the car and walked across E. 185th Street to the address of Amy's former employer—767 E. 185th Street. The former Red Robin was now a vacant store front that was for rent and in need of more than a little spit and polish. Most of the street was still vibrant with commerce and we parked in front of a barber shop where you could still get a hair cut for $7.00. As we were walking toward the former Red Robin store, a young man and his son were coming out of the barber shop making a memory—both the young man and his little boy had fresh hair cuts and they were laughing and brushing the tiny hairs off of their fresh summer buzz cuts.

My co-worker and I then walked from the former Red Robin store to the Sambula home and the murder scene. Mapquest indicated this would be a 28 second ride by automobile. As my co-worker and I continued walking I counted the paces—it is 300 paces from the former Red Robin store to the Sambula's former address at 18715 Pawnee. It was delightful July summer day. The birds were singing and children were playing in the neighborhood. The neighborhood seemed so alive and so full of life.

Ten feet and Amy would have been safe. Ten feet and Amy would have been shaking off the November chill and enjoying a Saturday dinner with her family. Ten feet and there would not have not been any subject matter for this book—but that was not meant to be. We started to play the what if's. What if Amy worked a little later that day or called off sick or left work a little earlier. Ten feet or ten minutes that was all it would have taken to spare Amy's life. That was not what God had planned.

As we left the scene of Amy's murder my co-worker and I were moved to silence. Both of us were taken back by the emotion that washed over us. Neither one of us could even begin to imagine the emotional pain that George and Joan went through so many years ago and that still tugs at George's heart today.

My co-worker asked if we could one day visit Amy's grave. She wondered what George and his wife would have put on Amy's headstone. I told my co-worker I would ask George if he would give us his permission to visit Amy's grave. When I saw George in church and told him about our road trip and asked him if we could see Amy's grave he said sure we could.

As we traveled along the shoreway back to Route 90 we passed a delivery truck with a Pegasus on the side as part if its logo. When we got back to the office my co-worker googled Pegasus meaning and definition. Google tells us that Pegasus was a winged horse fabled to have sprung from the body of Medusa when she was slain. Pegasus is noted for causing, with a blow from his hoof, Hippocrene, the inspiring fountain of the Muses, to spring from Mount Helicon. On this account Pegasus is, in modern times, associated with the Muses, and with ideas of poetic inspiration—just as Amelia is still inspiring others after over forty years since she last walked on the earth.

As my co-worker and I pulled off Route 90 onto E. 9th Street the sun was streaming into my old truck and she said to me with tears in her eyes it is not fair, "Amy's killer is out here somewhere enjoying a beautiful sunny day and she is dead." I explained to her that part of God's plan for George was to suffer the loss of both his young daughter and shortly thereafter his wife. I explained to my co-worker that God put George through these trials so that he could defeat alcoholism and also come to know Christ as his Lord and Savior. I explained to her that George fully understands what God put him through to be the man he is today and that George knows that there was no other way for him to defeat his addiction and have Christ as his Lord and Master.

My co-worker said that she wished she could see things like I do and it is my feverant prayer that one day she will.

CHAPTER TWENTY SIX

God Doesn't Discriminate

As for man, his days are like grass;
As a flower of the field, so he flourishes.
For the wind passes over it, and it is gone.
And its place remembers it no more.

Psalm 103:15-16

Come now, you who say "Today or tomorrow we
will go to such and such a city, spend a year there, buy and
sell and make a profit."

Whereas you do not know what will happen tomorrow.
For what is your life? It is even a vapor that appears
for a little time and vanishes.

James 4:13-14

People get ready there's a train a comin'
You don't need no ticket you just get on board

    From the song "People Get Ready" by Curtis Mayfield

I was sitting in the dentist's office a little while back and read an article on the death of Christina Green. This little girl was the victim of a random shooting directed at Congresswoman Gabrielle Giffords. This little girl was a 9/11 baby and happened to be born and die on two of America's darkest days almost ten years apart.

During a cool Saturday morning in Tucson, Arizona a madman began randomly shooting at 10:10 AM leaving in his wake fourteen persons wounded and six dead—including nine year old Christina Green, the daughter of John and Roxana Green. John is a baseball scout and the son of former major league baseball pitcher and baseball executive Dallas Green.

I am guessing that we could ask why the six victims, and why those six and why those six at this time in their lives. But that is not really the central question here. The more germane question here is that when death does end our lives will we be ready? Our Father will call every one of us to His side at one time or another. It is certainly His right to call us home. He brought us into this world and He certainly can return us to Himself. There is no question there. The question remains—will you be ready?

As tragic as this story may seem the fact of the matter is that our lives are that little dash on the gravestone between the day we are born and the day that we are called home to be with our heavenly Father. Every day across the world the obituaries are filled with names and faces of young and old from every nation and from every walk of life and from every creed and color to take that one final road trip back home. George and Carol and I and my wife and son are all waiting to board that long train home one day to be reunited with our Father and our loved ones. What a glorious reunion that will be. Will you be ready?

CHAPTER TWENTY SEVEN

Cousin Jerry

For unto us a Child is born . . . .
And His name will be called Wonderful Counselor,
Mighty God, Everlasting Father, Prince of Peace

Isaiah 9:6

On November 20, 2011 Pastor Majetich and I and two additional members of our Church, Ron Kent and Bud Grover, made our monthly evening trek to the Geauga County jail with the main purpose of giving a salvation message to those who need Christ in their lives. The county separates the men into two sections, those men who have committed felonies and those who have committed lesser misdemeanor crimes. Pastor Bob and I elected to provide music and a Bible lesson and a salvation message to the felony group.

After Pastor Bob had completed the evening message I knelt before the men and asked them to give me any of their prayer needs and I would pray for them on the spot (as well as take the prayer requests back to our Church). I then asked the men to close their eyes and asked each of them to raise their hands if they wished to now admit that they were sinners and invite Christ into their hearts. Two men raised their hands, and I invited both of them to come with me and recite the sinner's prayer and invite Christ into their hearts. Both men, Dan and Jerry, stepped forward and admitted than they were sinners and they both believed that Jesus had died for their sins and were ready to invite Christ into their hearts.

I was most struck by the story that Jerry told outlining the path that brought him to the jail that evening. Jerry had just been arrested for his umpteenth DUI (driving under the influence of alcohol) and he was now facing a prison term of three to four years. The Geauga County jail serves as a holding cell for state and federal prisoners who are awaiting sentencing to a state or federal facility. This would be the first time that Jerry was ever sentenced to a state facility and at age sixty-four he was more than a little nervous to say the least. Having just turned sixty a little while ago I could not imagine spending even one day in prison at my age and here Jerry was facing three to four years in a state facility.

Sometimes it is easy to leave the men behind when we exit the correctional facility and other times their stories stick with me for quite a while. Often times their lives become part of my prayer life. That was the case with Jerry. I just could not get him out of my thoughts. A man whose life was riddled with alcohol abuse is once again reaping what he had sowed—time in prison when he should have been planning his retirement in sunny Florida.

The following Sunday I was leading a Sunday school lesson and at the end of the lesson I asked the class to pray for Jerry. I hoped that his conversion to Christ was more than a jail house conversion. I asked each class member to pray for safety for Jerry and to pray that the Holy Spirit had entered his heart and that Jerry truly believed.

Suddenly Carol Sambula blurted out, "Hey, Jerry is my cousin". Both Carol and George went on to explain to the class that Carol's cousin Jerry has had a chronic alcohol problem for years and that he was arrested for being drunk and trying to find a way to go to the store to purchase more alcohol on a motorized bicycle. Both Carol and George shook their heads and chuckled over the lengths an alcoholic goes through to get just one more drink. Carol added that she had been witnessing to Jerry for years and perhaps this time Jerry had finally come to know Christ as his Lord and Savior.

We see God's hand at work here in a number of fronts. First of all, both Carol and George had long been released from the bonds of alcoholism through the grace and mercy of our loving God. Just the other day George was telling us about his Eastern European neighbors who often begin and end an outdoor event in their backyard with drinking. Often times they invite George over for a shot of this or that and George always politely declines. The neighbors seem a little miffed and can't understand why George won't have a drink or two with them in solidarity. George just explains to them that he just doesn't drink anymore. That seems foreign to them. The greatest thing here is that God has replaced Carol and George's love of alcohol with a love for Christ. Our Lord is their new drink of choice.

God will always help us find a way to circumvent temptation if we allow him to work in our lives. I had witnessed to a young man, Keith, in jail in December of 2011 who just arrived (once again) for having violated his parole by using drugs. Keith's drug of choice is heroine and he just couldn't seem to kick this habit. Keith indicated that he was a "church-going, born again believer" but that he could just not kick drugs. I told Keith and the men about my sin of choice and that I carried this sin with me for most of my adult Christian life. Once I finally decided that I was not going to take Christ with me into the various dens of iniquity that I had visited in person and on my computer that the desire for participating in this sin subsided (along with my prayer that God take this sin desire out of my heart). I told Keith that the next time he wanted to get high and as he was tying that piece of rubber around his arm to find a good vein that he was to imagine Christ's outstretched arm on the cross and that Keith was tying off one of Christ's veins. I also asked Keith that when he was sticking that needle into his own arm to imagine sticking that needle into the arm of his Lord and Savior. Keith's eyes welled up and you could see that I had given Keith something to think about. I pray for Keith daily that the Holy Spirit does convict him of his sin and that he returns to an addiction free life style.

God's plan for each of our lives is filled with purpose and direction. Nothing happens just because. Over thirty years ago neither Carol nor George nor I knew Jesus Christ as our Lord and Savior. Before the Spring of 2009 I had no idea that I would be writing this book. Before November 2011 I had no idea who Jerry was or that I would be witnessing to him. Before December 2011 I had no idea who Keith was or that the Holy Spirit would place in my heart the words that might provide Keith with an addiction free future. But God did. From before the sands of time to our final breath God knows our inner most being. He knows our very thoughts before we even think them. God has given us a Wonderful Counselor, a Mighty God, an Everlasting Father, and a Prince of Peace as seen in Isaiah 9:6. All we have to do is invite Him to reside in our hearts through His Son, Jesus.

CHAPTER TWENTY EIGHT

A Visit to Amy

"Sing praise to the Lord You saints of His,
And give thanks at the remembrance of
His holy name.

"For His anger is but for a moment,
His favor is for life;
Weeping may endure for a night,
But joy comes in the morning."

Psalm 30:4-5

Through the Lord's mercies we are not consumed,
Because his compassions fail not,
They are new every morning.

Lamentations 3:22-23

As the first snow was falling on greater Cleveland on December 7, 2011 my co-worker and I made our way to the gravesite of Amy to meet with George and Carol Sambula. We thought that as one of the final chapters in this book that it would be a fitting tribute to pay homage to the memory of Amy.

It would be George's 80th birthday in just a couple of days (December 9, 2011) and I am sure that his heart was filled with a multitude of thoughts and reflections as we approached George and Carol and followed them to Amy's graveside. As we approached the grave side the temperature was in the mid to low 30'S and you could tell that snow was just around the corner. It was an unusually mild start to the winter for Cleveland—normally we would be into several weeks of snow at this point in our winter weather season.

I introduced George and Carol to my co-worker and we walked over to Amy's grave. On the headstone was the inscription Beloved Daughter Amelia Theresa Sambula with the dates 2-20-52 to 11-22-69. At the bottom of the headstone were the words "Praise God" and on the upper left hand corner were a cross and a trumpet (Amy's favorite instrument). My co-worker and I could not imagine the pain that George and Joan suffered as they had to decide what words to place on their daughter's headstone.

Joan's headstone was next to Amy's with the last name Sambula on the top with Mother, Joan, and the dates 1933-75 in the right hand corner. "May they rest in peace" was noted on the bottom of the headstone with a place remaining for George's name. I said a prayer over both of the gravesides and my co-worker handed George and Carol a gift package for Christmas. My co-worker remarked what a coincidence it was that the wrapping paper she picked out had trumpets on it—Amy's favorite instrument. My co-worker remarked that she did not know how this happened and Carol said "We do" and she and George just smiled at each other knowing God's hand to be at work here.

As an aside here, I had been wrestling with the notion of retirement and had been praying to God for an answer to this question. As all four of us were leaving George remarked that his brother-in-law, a retired policeman, had come to visit Amy's grave ever since she was buried. George added that his brother-in-law had been retired for six weeks and died and never even got a chance to spend one retirement check. My co-worker just smiled at me and said there is your answer. Funny how God works . . . .

In the course of writing this book I asked George and Carol hundreds of questions in an effort to provide the readers with an exact portrayal of how each of them were feeling regarding their roles in bringing to light this book. In order to best capture the raw emotion of how George felt relative to the loss of both his daughter and his wife please find the actual question and answer session that was crafted after we visited the gravesides of both Amy and Joan.

Q. George, over the years have your feelings about visiting the grave of your daughter changed? How so?

A. Well, I think there is still a sadness and a heartbreak every time I go to Amelia's grave, the feeling is always sad. In the past when I would visit I cried more than I do now and sometimes I cried so much that I couldn't even pray over the gravesite. But as the years went on it seemed as if it lessoned, I don't have the crying now and I guess by this time I am all cried out. The tears are all gone but the feeling and the sadness never leaves me. It is only through the help of Jesus and the things that happened in my life after, that have helped me to grow more and more. Also the knowledge I have gained with the Lord has benefited me greatly in my life. I am ever grateful to the Lord Jesus Christ for being in my life. All the things I went through in my life are sort of ceasing and there is happiness in my life today. I had so many years of sadness that it took a long time to come out of it. It was only through faith in the Lord and His healing me that this happened.

Q. How about visiting the graveside of your wife, have those feeling changed over the years? How so?

A. It is the same when visiting my wife's grave. It was always sad to go and visit my wife's grave. The tears would come out so profusely that I would still be crying on my way back home. It seemed like the tears would never seem to cease until later, much later. As time went on and with God's healing, it amazes me how I have changed and my outlook has changed every time I visit the site and pray at the gravesite. As a Catholic I always went there and said the Our Father and the Hail Mary's and they sort of consoled me. And now as a real Christian, I still can't go there and say the words I would like to say. Sometimes the words just won't come out so I sometimes pray to the Lord when I get home in silence. It is easier for me to do it that way instead of standing over the grave site and praying. So there is still a sadness in my life and heart and there always will be. This is what happens when you lose family and your beautiful daughter who was so good in everything she did, especially in school and playing a musical instrument. She honored God in all she did. But at the time of her death it was a little easier because I had my wife with me, but when my wife died I had nobody but my lonely self. It was a very hard time in my life to go through and as I was a drinker my alcoholism seemed to progress much faster than it would have probably if these things hadn't happened in my life.

Q. They say that time heals all wounds, does that seem to be the case here. It goes without saying that the pain you felt in 1969 must have been immense. Has that pain diminished over the years? How so? If the pain has diminished to what do you attribute this?

A. As time goes on it does become easier but the pain and sorrow are always there. I attribute this healing to knowing Jesus and I think through Him all things are possible. It means an awful lot to me to be associated to Jesus Christ.

Q. I imagine that back in the early years of Amy's death you probably felt like dying yourself. It must have been tough even to get out of bed and get dressed and go to work. What kept you going?

A. When Amy first died it was a very hard thing to face, I was very bitter toward who did it and I felt, why me Lord? I was blaming everything and everybody. I was suspicious of everything and everybody. Getting through this time in our lives was a very tough thing to do. Just a wasted thing that somebody would take a persons life for no reason at all. It never did come out in the trial why this guy took her life. Whether he was trying to drag her in the bushes or molest her or she refused him, we don't know. There was no evidence of any molestation. It was almost a guilt feeling on our part, why, why, why did this happen? The answers didn't come and we just couldn't understand. We had a lot of people in our lives and family praying for us. I still had to be tough and get out of bed, get dressed and go to work. I had to be there for my wife and the rest of my family. We still had to function as a family. I guess it just came natural to go out and do what you had to do. But we were really blessed with a lot of people trying to help in that situation. As I look back now it was really a trying time and I don't know how I got through it. I wished I had died instead because my daughter had such a love for life and a love for everything she did. Whatever she did in school or with the other girls made it such a blessing to go and hear her play solo with her trumpet or to watch her perform in other areas. I cherish all those things and when you look back on the years with her it was just a blessing that God let us have her for the time we did have with her. I was truly blessed to have a daughter of her magnitude, her love and her understanding of everything. A daughter who knew Jesus and lived to show the love of Christ in all she did. I was truly blessed.

Q. Again, the pain of losing your wife some six years later must had been equally intense? Has this pain diminished over the years? How so? To what do you attribute this?

A. As hard as it was to lose my daughter it was even harder when I lost my wife six years later. When I lost my daughter I still had my wife and we could console each other. We went through all the pain, crying, tears and heartbreak together. I had a partner in all the pain. But when she died, I had nobody and I couldn't go to the kids. At that time there were no bereavement groups to go to. As far as I knew there was nowhere to go to get help. It was the hardest thing I ever suffered in my life. My addiction to alcohol got worse and worse with this. I was getting sick every time I drank and I needed the alcohol just to exist. I needed the alcohol to get up in the morning and to be able to go to work and get through the day. It probably helped me because it numbed me and brought me to a place where I had to get help with my alcoholism. Time does help heal all wounds and it did help to diminish the pain over the years. As time went on I met Carol and we started to date, it was a new life for me all over again. The kids were all about done with school and so it took a lot of the pain away at that time. I also learned in AA that you had to turn it all over to God. I had been a Catholic all of my life and I believed that God was with me. Many times I asked God "Why me, God? I couldn't understand why this happened. I had not yet received the Lord Jesus Christ as my savior but I believed in God and His love for me. I think having the other children were a blessing in my life also because they helped get me through it some how. Learning more about AA and then learning more about Jesus was a stepping stone. It was a long process but one thing led to another and everything just started coming into place. It all helped to straighten my life out and if it hadn't, I would be dead today because I was at a point of no return. It is hard to describe the mental and physical pain I went through. It is only through the love of God that I came out of this and I am eternally grateful.

Q. Again, with the loss of Joan once again it must have been tough to even get through the day? What kept you going?

A. I guess that is really what kept me going, knowing I had to take care of my children. It was a tearful time in my life and I cried myself to sleep many nights. I had nobody to console me or to turn to. Just part of you is gone when you lose your wife. I had wished God had taken me instead.

Q. With either the loss of Amy or Joan did you ever contemplate just ending it all and going to join them? What stopped you?

A. I never really ever contemplated ending my life, although I wished I had been the one to die. Alcohol numbed me and helped me get through it all. I know it was hard for the kids to see how alcohol got the best of me. I needed alcohol morning, noon and night just to exist. I knew there had to be a better way to live so on my own I tried to quit three times without success. I finally made a decision to get help and I went into Rosary Hall for treatment at St. Vincent Charity Hospital in downtown Cleveland. It started me on a new path and a new way of life. Everything that was put in front of me was a stepping stone to a new and better life, a life of bettering myself, helping other people and then finding Jesus. I became very active in AA and I did help a lot of people.

Q. Did you see alcohol as an answer to your pain in the early days?

A. Yes, I used alcohol constantly in my life to get rid of my pain.

Q. What role has your salvation played in easing your pain?

A. I am so thankful that I do have Jesus in my life. In my early days I wanted to be the "Man" doing things my way, being my own man. Believing you could do anything you wanted to do, do it my way, you know? But my way wasn't always the right way. So I found out I needed somebody else in my life, Jesus my Lord, He was my answer. I learned how to know Him, love Him and depend on Him for an awful lot. Not my own will, but His will, His will be done. It took a lot of pain, suffering and crying in my life to bring me to this place. I am just thankful that I have Carol in my life and that she led me to the Lord. She knew about Him and had known Him several years when we met. She was just happy to help my whole family come to know the Lord. She has led most of them to the Lord and she is still working on a lot of it. So I have been blessed to have two women in my life. Usually a man only has one wife all his life but I've been very fortunate that because of the death of my first wife I have a second wife. Which I am very pleased and thankful for. I just appreciate everything Jesus has done for me, I have been blessed just knowing Him.

Q. When my co-worker and I asked to see Amy's grave how did that make you feel? What were your thoughts as we stood there looking at the grave? What were your thoughts when we prayed?

A. When we prayed it was a blessing to hear you pray, Dan. It's an uplift to hear prayer anytime. It just uplifts me very much. I don't know how Carol felt but I know it inspired me. I am so blessed to have you in my life, Dan, and to have your co-worker helping you. Carol and I are both so blessed to have you in our lives.

CHAPTER TWENTY-NINE

The Beginning

My sheep hear My voice, and I know them, and they follow Me.

John 10:27

Most books close with some sort of an ending—but not this book. The final chapter is not an ending but a beginning. You might have picked up this book out of curiosity or out of boredom or perhaps you have some unresolved issues with God. Maybe you have suffered the loss of a loved one and are angry with God in that He took somebody away from you that was very special to you and that you have issues with either Him or His Son or both of them. There is no doubt that if you have suffered the loss of a loved one that your pain is real and that the loss you have endured is so painful at times that you just don't know how you will get through to the next day—but you will.

There is no doubt that God is aware of your pain and anguish and that He and His Son are with you every step of the way. Hebrews 12:11 says the following:

> Now no chastening seems joyful for the present, but painful; nevertheless, afterward it yields the peaceable fruit of righteousness to those who have been trained by it. NKJ

I am not saying that the loss of a loved one is chastening by God—what I am saying is that God is in control and for whatever reason He has elected to bring a particular circumstance into your life. Whether it is a health issue or a financial issue or an emotional issue, God has elected to place this roadblock in your particular path of life.

I happened to be in Charlottesville, Virginia recently on business on the last Sunday on August of 2011 and I drove over to my wife's home church, Fork Union Baptist Church in Fork Union, Virginia. Fork Union is a sleepy little southern town 40 miles or so east of Charlottesville. The town's claim to fame is that it is the home of the Fork Union Military Academy.

Pastor Warren Johnson delivered an excellent sermon on the security and assurance of our salvation. Pastor Johnson was kind enough to give me a copy of his sermon which is in part the basis and motivation for this final chapter. Just before starting his sermon Pastor Johnson asked that we pray for the family of a teenage girl who had been recently killed in a one car automobile accident shortly before she was to head off to her freshman year in college.

In addition to asking for our prayers for the family of this young girl Pastor Johnson asked the following question—if you knew that in fifteen minutes you would die, would you not want to make sure that you would wake up in heaven with the Lord? He further asked would you say to yourself I don't know what God is going to say—welcome home, child or depart from me I never knew you.

Pastor Johnson made it very clear in his sermon that God is indeed God and that He cannot lie as seen in the following passage from Titus 1:1-2:

1. Paul, a bondservant of God, and an apostle of Jesus Christ, according to the faith of God's elect and the acknowledgement of the truth which accords to godliness,

2. In hope of eternal life which God, who cannot lie, promised before time began.

God does not make mistakes. If God says that he has promised us eternal life then it is so—he cannot lie.

Again in Timothy we see that we have been promised eternal life and that this promise has been given made to us before the beginning of time:

8. Therefore do not be ashamed of the testimony of our Lord, nor of me His prisoner, but share with me in the sufferings for the gospel according to the power of God,

9. who has saved us and called us with a holy calling, not according to our works, but according to His own purpose and grace which was given to us in Christ Jesus before time began.

Again we can see in 2 Timothy 1:8-9 that God was concerned about the salvation of each and every one of us before we even begin to draw our first breath.

The following Sunday (September 4, 2011) I again found myself at my wife's home church. I had actually planned on sleeping in that Sunday morning but found myself being led to the service once again. I saw in the bulletin for September 4th that under the prayer list section that it was noted that the love and sympathy of the Fork Union Baptist Church is with the family of Allison Buck (the young lady who was mentioned in last week's service as having been killed in a one car accident). It was announced in the bulletin that her funeral was held at the Fork Union church on Tuesday, August 30 and she was buried at Fork Union Baptist Memorial Cemetery.

I could not help but have been struck by the terrible irony here. As I was just finishing up on the book relative to the life and death of Amelia Sambula and the subsequent impact on George Sambula another chapter was opening in the lives of the Buck family as they had just buried their daughter. I could not help but think that at this very moment in time new chapters regarding the loss of a precious son or daughter were being opened across our nation and throughout the world.

As I was thinking and scribbling down additional notes for the book Pastor Johnson directed us to John 11 where we find Jesus deeply moved to tears over the loss of his dear friend, Lazarus. We find in this chapter that in addition to Jesus weeping (verse 35) that his sorrow actually caused Him to groan in verse 38 despite the fact that He knew that He would be raising His dear friend from the dead shortly.

Pastor Johnson then directed us to the following verses (John 11:41-44)

> 41. Then they took away the stone from the place where the dead man was lying. And Jesus lifted His eyes and said, "Father, I thank you that you have heard Me.
>
> 42. And I know that You always hear Me, but because of the people who are standing by I said this, that they may believe You sent Me.
>
> 43. Now when He had said these things, He cried with a loud voice, "Lazarus, come forth!"
>
> 44. And he who had died came out bound hand and foot with graveclothes, and his face was wrapped with a cloth. Jesus said to them, "Loose him, and let him go."

Here we see two paramount truths in verses 41 and 43. In verse 41 we find that God does hear our prayers (just as he heard those of His Son) and God does answer them. In verse 43 we find that Jesus does have power over life and death and through His resurrection He has defeated death as illustrated through the resurrection of Lazarus (as well as the reappearance of Jesus on earth after His dying on the cross).

For those of us who have invited Christ into our lives, the trials that we face should be overshadowed by the truth that one day we will receive our eternal reward. That should be enough to overcome the trials that we face here on earth. This is quite evident in the following passage from I John 2:25 and 1 John 5:13

> And this is the promise that He has promised us—eternal life (I John 2:25)

> These things I have written to you who believe in the name of the Son of God, that you may know that you have eternal life, and that you may continue to believe in the name of the Son of God (I John 5:13)

But at times when the circumstances of life surround us on all sides and seem to close in on us this eternal promise seems to pale when we are confronted with life itself.

As I was sitting back in my home church with my wife on Sunday September 18, 2011 I was struck by the fact that two families, the Reilly family and the Whitcomb family, who had experienced the loss of their sons so many years ago, were in the same Sunday service both calling on God to enter into their lives once again. As our Pastor, Robert Majetich, asked for additional prayer requests during the Sunday service one of our elders, Dick Whitcomb, asked that we pray for his sister Jean in Florida. Jean had lost her husband in November of 2010 and Jean's daughter had just lost her life. We then were asked to pray for safety for Brett Reilly who was being deployed to Afghanistan. Brett's parents, Bruce and Marcia Reilly, had buried Brett's older brother Sean seven years ago. The fact remains that from the time of their initial losses to today, God had not left their sides. He and His loving Son have been with them every step of the way providing love and comfort to them as that continued their journey to their eternal home. God has been there to provide a single beam of light for each and every one of us during our darkest hours here on earth. Time and time again God has provided and will continue to provide that ray of hope which will illuminate our way out of the darkest abyss of our lives—the help is there—all we have to do is ask.

It is my sincere hope, as well as the hope of George and Carol Sambula, that you will be able to use lessons learned in the lives of George and his family that God is indeed a loving and caring God. God does not make mistakes and we are all His creation and he wants the very best for each and every one of us. Once we receive His Son, Jesus into our hearts then we are His children as we see in John 1:12 which states that "but as many as received Him, to them He gave the right to become children of God, *even* to those who believe in His name."

As we close here take a moment and reflect on the following closing verses from John 10:26-30:

> 26. But you do not believe, because you are not of My sheep, as I said to you.

27. My sheep hear My voice, and I know them and they follow me.

28. And I give them eternal life, and they shall never perish; neither shall anyone snatch them out of my hand.

27. My Father, who has given them to Me, is greater than all; and no one is able to snatch them out of My Father's hand.

28. I and My Father are one.

For those of you who know Christ as your Lord and Savior, think back to a time when you did not hear His voice—during your period of unbelief. Recall those times and count the multitude of blessings you have received from your salvation onward. No matter what trials you are facing today our tomorrow is already set for us in glory.

For those of you who have not yet made a decision to invite Christ into your hearts the time is not too late. At this moment as you are closing the final chapter in this book you can recite the following simple prayer:

> Lord, I know that I am a sinner. I know that Christ died for my sins. I believe that Jesus is my Lord and Savior and I invite Him into my heart.

Romans 10:9 tells us that if you have confessed your sin with your mouth and believed with your heart you will be saved.

George, Carol and I pray that you will be blessed by reading the story of George and how the tragedy in his life has turned to victory in Christ. We thank you for taking time to read this book and hope that the words we have crafted bring you peace and inspiration. We thank God for the inspiration to bring this book to light and give Him the praise and glory as witnessed in these writings. We would like to close with the chorus from the song "He Knows My Name":

He knows my name,
He knows my every thought.
He sees each tear that falls,
And He hears me when I call.

May these words provide comfort to you in your time of need. Amen . . . .

Edwards Brothers Malloy
Thorofare, NJ USA
September 18, 2013